TIKAL, CITY OF THE MAYA

TIKAL,
CITY OF THE MAYA

James and Oliver Tickell

Photographs by Francesco Venturi

Tauris Parke Books, London

'Here were the remains of a cultivated, polished, and peculiar people who had past through all the stages incident to the rise and fall of nations; reached their golden age, and perished, entirely unknown. The links which connected them with the human family were severed and lost, and these were the only memorials of their footsteps upon earth. We lived in the ruined palaces of their kings; we went up their desolate temples and fallen altars; and wherever we moved, we saw the evidences of their taste, their skill in arts, their wealth and power.'
(John Stephens, *Incidents of Travel in Central America*, 1848)

This book is dedicated to the modern Maya peoples, conquered but not defeated.

The authors and photographer would like to thank the following for their help in the production of this book: Zita Palkovits, Dr Erwin Blandon (H. E. the Guatemalan Ambassador to the UK), the Housing Corporation.

Published by Tauris Parke Books
110 Gloucester Avenue, London NW1 8JA
in association with KEA Publishing Services Ltd, London

Text © 1991 James Tickell and Oliver Tickell
Photographs © 1991 Francesco Venturi/KEA

TRAVEL TO LANDMARKS
Series Editor: Judy Spours
Editorial Assistant: Elizabeth Harcourt
Designers: Holdsworth Associates
Maps by: András Bereznay

All photographs by Francesco Venturi except pages 48 (left), 61 (below), 83 (below right), 97 (right) by James Tickell; pages 49, 51 (above), 62 (below left), 63 (below right), 89 (right), 109, 115 (above) by Oliver Tickell.

The Cataloguing in Publication data for this book is available from the British Library.

ISBN 1-85043-233-6

Photosetting by Litho Link Ltd, Welshpool, Powys, UK
Colour separations by Fabbri, Milan, Italy
Printed by Fabbri, Milan, Italy

Frontispiece The face of Tikal's Stela 31, dated AD 445, showing the distinguished ruler Stormy Sky, who greatly expanded Tikal's imperial domain. The ruler's face has been slightly defaced, but the full detail of his magnificent head-dress and ornaments have been well preserved. In his right hand he is holding up a chain of office; on his left arm is the head of the sun god, with Tikal's emblem glyph on the god's head-dress. The stela was found in 1960, built into Stormy Sky's funerary temple on the North Acropolis, and now stands in Tikal's Visitors' Centre.

Contents

Introduction

In the year AD 768, Charlemagne was crowned King of the Franks amid great ceremonies, heralding the end of the Dark Ages in Europe, the revival of the Holy Roman Empire, and the defeat of the Arab threat to Christendom. At the same time but far away, among towering pyramids in the tropical jungles of modern Guatemala, Chitam became ruler of Tikal and its domain. His people no doubt celebrated the event with intricate and splendid rituals, perhaps even with human sacrifice, but at this we can only guess. Both men ruled for the best part of fifty years, unaware of each other's existence as if on different planets. Unlike Charlemagne, however, Chitam's rule was an end and not a beginning. Foreign invaders were closing in on Tikal, Chitam's empire was fragmenting, and the great civilization of the Classic Maya was entering an eternal night.

Over 1,000 years after the fall of Tikal, the five great pyramid temples still rise up above the surrounding trees. Jungle creepers entwine their stairways, the once brightly painted stucco facings have long fallen away to reveal the crumbling limestone beneath. Tikal is one of the great ruins of the world. It not only stands as a monument to a civilization which rose and fell in the distant past, but provides key evidence for modern understanding of the Classic Maya.

Tikal was the pinnacle of Maya civilization and cultural achievement, with its Golden Age between the third and ninth centuries AD, exactly the time of the Dark Ages in Europe. This was the Classic Period of Mesoamerica, that region between the southern United States down to the Isthmus of Panama, the only area of North America where major indigenous civilizations emerged (see map on page 8). The ruins that we see today at Tikal date from the Maya Classic period; they represent the highest achievement of Maya architecture, the most enduring and most impressive of Maya artistic expressions, and were fundamental to the Maya world order.

Many people have seen the ruins of Tikal without realising it. In the film *Star Wars*, the city features as a rebel stronghold at the far end of the universe, the pyramids acting as shelters for the rebuilding of battle-damaged space cruisers. The role is appropriate enough; until the brutal shock of the Spanish Conquest in the early sixteenth century, the story of civilization in the Americas is indeed quite separate from the rest of mankind. Better known than the Maya are the later Precolumbian civilizations that fought great battles against the Spanish, the Aztecs of

Eastern part of the North Terrace and Acropolis at Tikal, seen over the Great Plaza, the ceremonial heart of the city. The thatched covers protect stone altars and stelae (carved tablets) from the rain and sun. The twelve temples of the Acropolis were built again and again, each time becoming more magnificent. Their main purpose seems to have been the veneration of ancestors, as nearly 100 funeral chambers have been discovered under the structures.

Right Detail of façade at the Nunnery Quadrangle at Uxmal, in Mexico's Yucatán peninsula, showing the head of a warrior or god. Uxmal flourished in the Early Postclassic era (AD 800-1000), reaching its height after the mysterious fall of Tikal. Its sophisticated 'Puuc' style of architecture rivals the artistic achievements of the Classic period.

the Valley of Mexico, and the Incas in the Andes mountains of South America.

Before the Conquest a mosaic of different cultures existed in Mesoamerica, rising and declining over millennia, conquering and being conquered. The great multitude of names archaeologists use to describe and date Mesoamerican societies often seem confusing, although the cultural patterns show strong continuity throughout the periods. There is general agreement on the names for the four main eras in Mesoamerica, the Archaic, the Preclassic, the Classic, and the Postclassic leading up to the Conquest, and this is the frame of reference used in this book (see chronology on page 125).

The Maya play a major part in each of these eras, and within Mesoamerica they were by far the most advanced civilization in terms of art and architecture, and the sciences of astronomy and calculation of dates. The complex Maya calendar was more accurate than calendars in use in Europe at the same time, and was the main spring of

Overleaf Tikal's Temple I, the Temple of the Great Jaguar, at dusk with the evening shadows lengthening over the North Acropolis to the left. The heavily eroded front of the roof-comb shows a seated figure and serpent – just discernible with an effort of the imagination.

their religion and science. The Maya flourished in different phases for more than fifteen centuries, covering a far greater area and timespan than any other Mesoamerican culture. At their greatest extent, they covered a large part of Mesoamerica, including south-western Mexico, Guatemala, Belize, and parts of Honduras and Salvador. This was never a unitary empire, but a collection of city states under the control of dynastic families, linked by trade and marriage alliances.

The Maya territory divides into four culturally distinct areas, again referred to throughout this book. The first is the Guatemalan highlands, part of the mountainous backbone of both American continents; this saw the first Preclassic Maya flowering, with a major centre at Kaminaljuyu near modern Guatemala City. South of the highlands is the Pacific coastal zone, which is relatively unexplored, but played an important part in earlier Maya development. The third area is the central lowlands, which include the Petén rainforest and Tikal, the centre of Maya civilization during the Classic era. Also within the central lowlands is the coastal zone of the Gulf of Mexico, now being recognised as an area of key importance at the end of the Classic era. Finally, there are the flat and dry northern lowlands of the Yucatán peninsula, which became the focus of Maya civilization during the Postclassic era, after the fall of Tikal.

The Maya peoples live on today, still forming more than half of the population of the old Maya area. Undoubtedly they are the descendants of Tikal's builders; the faces of the Maya workmen at Tikal today are the same as those that look out from the stelae, carved monuments that served as Tikal's dynastic record. The Maya today live in poverty within the dominant Spanish speaking society, their culture and languages surviving, but the achievement of their ancestors no more than the echo of a memory.

The mystery of Tikal's fall has long preoccupied Mayanists. Until recently, archaeologists have sought to explain this in terms of apocalyptic events, wars, volcanic eruptions, pandemics and famines. It is now clear, however, that although catastrophes may have played a part, complex social and environmental factors were at work, leading to a more gradual collapse whereby the delicate balance of survival that long supported Tikal was eventually shattered. A greater mystery still is how such a great city could have existed in such difficult tropical conditions, especially in a society that did not use the wheel or beasts of burden. The question of how the Maya sustained their cities is one that archaeologists have answered only in part, and highlights the gaps in our knowledge. New scientific modelling techniques, combining traditional archaeology with ecology, botany and nutritional studies are only now beginning to yield results.

The story of Maya civilization continues beyond the Spanish Conquest, finally being completed with the overthrow of the last independent Maya outpost at Tayasal, near Tikal, in 1697. Perhaps the real end came one day in July 1562 at Maní in the Yucatán peninsula of Mexico, when Bishop Diego de Landa ordered the collection and burning of all the Maya painted manuscripts and works of art that could be found. It was the funeral pyre of a civilization going back as far as 4,000 years. Science, astronomy, history, religion and art went up in smoke, condemned as 'superstitions and falsehoods of the devil'. Throughout the colonial period, Maya ruins and achievements were ignored, to be rediscovered by nineteenth-century Western explorers.

Maya studies have evolved since then to become an increasingly active field. Knowledge of events and people in Maya history is becoming more detailed. At the same time, new threats to the preservation of the ruins have emerged, with their roots in poverty, instability, and lack of investment. But for all the worries and theories, we can only hope to comprehend dimly the ancient Maya, how they lived and died, what they believed, what moved them to anger or happiness. To be at Tikal is to feel a sense of wonder at the ruins of this monumental city from a thousand years ago, and in a quiet moment to feel a distant human kinship with its vanished creators.

Imaginary low aerial view of Tikal, looking north-west over the site. The artist was an American, Carlos Vierra, and the painting is one of a series showing Maya ruins, painted in the early years of the twentieth century. The painting is remarkably accurate, given that the site was completely overgrown at time of painting. Even today, trees and jungle growth would almost entirely obscure the chosen line of sight. To the left of the picture is the enormous Palace Reservoir, on the south side of the Central Acropolis. Temples I and II are at the centre, and further to the right are the temples of the North Acropolis. *Photograph by Peter Harrison, courtesy San Diego Museum of Man.*

1 The Thousand Years of Tikal

Maya Spring

The beginning of the Maya world, the date 0.0.0.0.0 in their Long Count calendar, fell in the year 3114 BC, beginning a great cycle due to end in AD 2012, when the date would return to 0.0.0.0.0. We do not know what mythical events the Maya attributed to that starting date. Nor do we know what ominous predictions for the end of the cycle were made by the Maya priests, lords of the sacred cycles of time.

The calendar and the cycles of time were at the centre of the Maya world view. The Maya did not think of time as a series of never-repeated events, as we do, but as an interlocking hierarchy of recurring cycles, in which history and prophecy are mingled. Time itself was a Maya god, worshipped through the intricate calculations and observances of the three different calendrical systems that were in simultaneous use, joined together like the cogs of a wheel to chart eternity (see page 52).

We have little knowledge of the Maya area in 3114 BC. This pre-dates any evidence of village settlements and agriculture, which can first be established at around 2000 BC, the date for maize pollen found in cores of sediment from Lake Peténxil near Tikal. But the area was certainly inhabited. The first ancestors of the Maya were among the bands of hunter-gatherers who crossed into the Americas from the mainland of Asia some time between 50,000 and 30,000 BC, the exact date being hotly disputed by archaeologists.

People thought to have spoken an early Maya language first settled in villages along the Pacific coast as early as 2500 BC. They were among the earliest American peoples to adopt a settled way of life, based on the slash-and-burn cultivation of maize and other plants. By 2000 BC, the area of Maya settlement had spread up the major rivers into the interior, with the larger villages built around stone temples.

Despite the early Maya presence, the first major civilization to emerge in Mesoamerica was the Olmec, a sophisticated society led by warrior priests in the swampy coastal regions by the Gulf of Mexico. In many ways, it set the pattern for other civilizations to follow, including the Maya, and is often referred to as the mother culture of Mesoamerica. The Olmecs had trading links that stretched across the Maya area to the Pacific coast, south to modern El Salvador, and north into the Mexican highlands.

The roof-comb of Tikal's tallest structure, the 208-foot Temple IV, seen through jungle foliage. It was completed in AD 741 under the rule of Yax Kin, and unlike other temples at Tikal may not have been built over earlier structures. The path in the foreground follows the route of a wide ceremonial avenue, now overgrown, which linked Temple IV with the Great Plaza.

Almost nothing is known of the Olmec language or origins, but archaeological evidence shows that they carved stone altars and bas-reliefs in temples built on raised stone platforms, and created sophisticated ceramics and jewellery of precious stones. They are perhaps best known for the huge monolithic heads with pronounced negroid features that are associated with their temples. Most significantly, they devised a complex calendar from astronomical observation which underpinned their religion, mathematics and science. The Olmecs reached their height of achievement around 1000 BC in the Mesoamerican Preclassic era, contemporary with the biblical King Solomon of Israel. Decline then set in, followed by their apparent disappearance.

With the waning of Olmec power, three distinct centres of gravity were emerging in Mesoamerica, Teotihuacán in the Valley of Mexico, the Zapotecs in the Valley of Oaxaca, and the Maya in the south-west. These were to become the three major civilizations of Mesoamerica's Classic era, which lasted from AD 250 to 900.

Before the flowering of the Classic Maya period came the time known as the Late Preclassic. As early as 500 BC various distinctive Maya cultures were flourishing in different parts of the Maya area. Izapan civilization, named after Izapa in the modern state of Chiapas, Mexico, formed a vital link with the Olmec. Although most Izapan monuments date from the Late Preclassic, the culture had been active since Olmec times, and evidence of their early activities is found almost as far west as the Olmec area.

In the Guatemalan highlands, the Preclassic city of Kaminaljuyu (on the western outskirts of modern Guatemala City) had emerged as a dominant centre, and as the main rival to Izapa. The sophisticated ceramics and sculpture of its Miraflores people, as they are known, were far in advance of its Maya neighbours of the time.

The Preclassic Maya of the tropical lowlands, named after the Chicanel ceramics with which they are associated, were hardly less active. Only recently, with the discovery and partial excavation of some major late Preclassic sites in the northern lowlands, has the scope of their achievements been appreciated. Nowhere is this better illustrated than at El Mirador, a huge Preclassic city some 40 miles north of Tikal.

The distinguished Mayanist Michael Coe has described El Mirador as 'the oldest Maya capital city, far in advance of Tikal, which it dwarfs

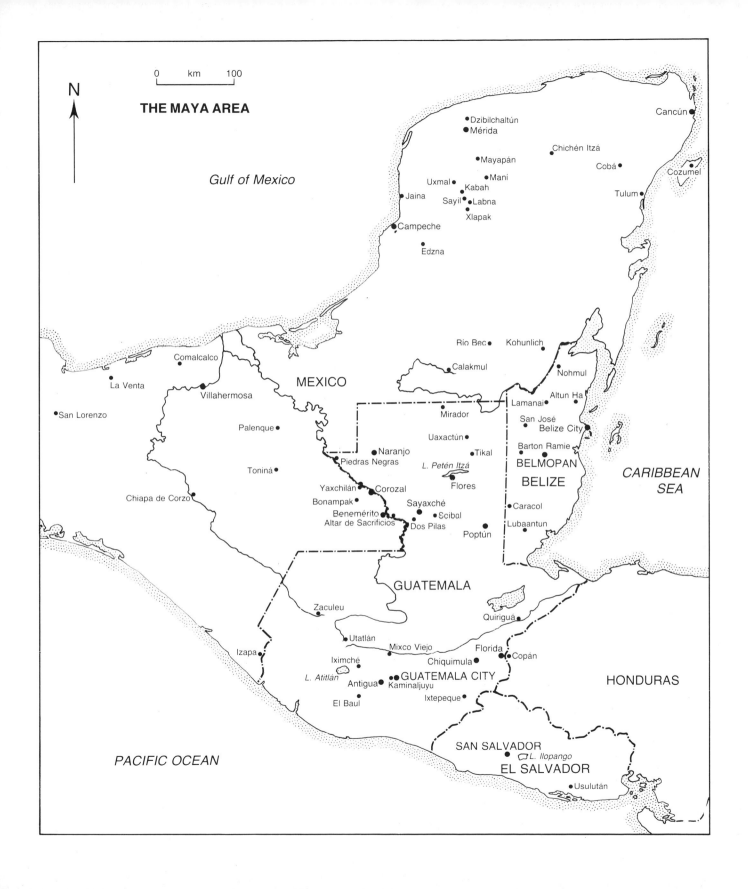

THE MAYA AREA

0 km 100

N

Gulf of Mexico

PACIFIC OCEAN

CARIBBEAN SEA

MEXICO

GUATEMALA

BELIZE

BELMOPAN

HONDURAS

EL SALVADOR

SAN SALVADOR

- Dzibilchaltún
- Mérida
- Cancún
- Chichén Itzá
- Mayapán
- Cobá
- Cozumel
- Maní
- Uxmal
- Kabah
- Jaina
- Sayil
- Labna
- Tulum
- Xlapak
- Campeche
- Edzna
- Río Bec
- Kohunlich
- Calakmul
- Nohmul
- Comalcalco
- Mirador
- Altun Ha
- Lamanai
- La Venta
- Villahermosa
- San José
- Belize City
- San Lorenzo
- Palenque
- Uaxactún
- Barton Ramie
- Naranjo
- Tikal
- Piedras Negras
- L. Petén Itzá
- Toniná
- Chiapa de Corzo
- Yaxchilán
- Corozal
- Flores
- Bonampak
- Sayaxché
- Caracol
- Benemérito
- Seibal
- Altar de Sacrificios
- Dos Pilas
- Lubaantun
- Poptún
- Zaculeu
- Quiriguá
- Utatlán
- Mixco Viejo
- Florida
- Izapa
- Iximché
- Chiquimula
- Copán
- L. Atitlán
- Antigua
- GUATEMALA CITY
- El Baul
- Kaminaljuyu
- Ixtepeque
- L. Ilopango
- Usulután

Left Temple 32 in Tikal's North Acropolis, the late afternoon sunshine giving a golden glow to the grey limestone. The burial chamber located under this Late Classic temple has not been identified with a particular individual, but he was clearly of some importance, as evidenced by the lavish offerings found.

Above right A volcano, dormant but not extinct, rising up over Lake Atitlán in the Guatemalan highlands. At the time of the Spanish Conquest, this area was dominated by warlike Maya peoples, who bitterly resisted the invaders. To this day, the local Maya resist integration with the Spanish-speaking culture and remain a subject people, with many of their towns and villages under military occupation.

Below right View of Temple II and the North Acropolis. Temple 33, at the centre front of the North Acropolis (right of picture), was rebuilt three times. The latest version was as large as Temple II, but was beyond repair and therefore dismantled by archaeologists during the 1960s. Only the bottom few steps of the stairway remain, and can clearly be seen here. The visible structure dates from the Early Classic period. At the top of the Temple II stairway, over to the left, the protruding stone block was probably used as a reviewing stand for rulers or priests to gaze down on the assembled company in the Great Plaza.

by its size and lessens by its antiquity'. Its main pyramid covers an area of 43 acres together with its surrounding platforms, and reaches a height of 230 feet to make it by some way the tallest known Maya building. The monumental constructions are connected by causeways, which radiate out towards secondary centres in the jungle.

Archaeologists now believe that El Mirador was the greatest Maya centre of its time, perhaps even on a par with Teotihuacán. It was certainly the primary focus of civilization for the entire central lowlands. The site has still only been partially excavated, and clues as to its development and history are eagerly awaited by Mayanists. There is no doubt that El Mirador played a role ancestral to Tikal, but the reasons for the collapse of El Mirador at the close of the Preclassic period and Tikal's subsequent rise remain obscure.

In Tikal the history of human settlement can be traced as far back as 700–500 BC, with a type of ceramic known as Eb. The first signs of major construction, which lie far beneath the superimposed Classic period constructions, date from the Late Preclassic. It is reasonable to suppose that Tikal, along with other contemporary centres such as Uaxactún, was dominated by El Mirador during this period.

After the Volcano

Some time between AD 200 and 250, the volcano of Ilopango erupted with such ferocity as to obliterate itself, leaving only the broad crater where the city of San Salvador now stands. The explosion was of a cataclysmic scale ranking with the impact of the Siberian meteor, or the eruption of Krakatoa, and releasing the power of many hundred nuclear bombs.

Everywhere within a wide radius of Ilopango became uninhabitable, buried under a deep layer of volcanic ash. Trade routes along the Pacific coast were cut off, and the fisheries on which coastal populations depended were devastated. For several centuries, Maya civilization along the Pacific and in the southern highlands was destroyed. By the time that recovery became possible, the area was controlled by Teotihuacán. Until its eventual decline and fall around AD 600, Teotihuacán was to remain the major influence throughout Meso-america, with trading colonies in all parts of the Maya area.

With the eruption of Ilopango and the disappearance of centres throughout the southern highlands and along the Pacific coast, a

The front of Stela 9 at Tikal, now in the Visitors' Centre at the site. It shows Kan Boar, who was ruling at Tikal in AD 475, holding a staff or spear, a symbol of office. As with many stelae, his face has been defaced, probably a ritual action after the death of a ruler. Unlike later carvings, the style of this carving is austere, with the ruler standing out against an uncluttered background.

Above The recently restored Late Preclassic Pyramid of the Lost World, in the south-western part of Tikal. With a 100-foot square plan, the pyramid was vast for its time. There is no trace of a temple, although it may have carried a perishable structure of wood with a thatched palm roof. The pyramid had a stairway on each side flanked by large masks, the most important being on the west (seen here).

Overleaf The North Acropolis, with Temple 1's nine terraces and central stairway to the right of the picture. The temple stairway was in fact a construction stair used by labourers to carry up building material. It was built over at the final stage with larger steps for ceremonial use, but only the bottom few of these have survived.

realignment of power took place throughout the Maya area, to the advantage of the northern lowlands. The main north-south trade moved inland from the Pacific coast to the lowland rivers, bringing economic growth, and opening up new areas for colonization. A large-scale population shift into the lowlands also took place, favouring some centres and undermining others. Ilopango's eruption marked the beginning of the Classic period of Maya civilization.

For reasons we do not know, El Mirador was a disastrous loser, while Tikal was a clear winner in the post-Ilopango order. The first dynastic monument of the lowlands, Stela 29 at Tikal, dates from AD 292, just 40–90 years after Ilopango's eruption. This monument bears the first example of Tikal's emblem glyph (the equivalent perhaps of a European coat of arms), a symbol whose power was to endure for over six centuries.

This shows that Tikal had by that time established its independence as a primary centre in its own right. The name of the ruler whose stylized image is carved on the stela is Scroll Ahau Jaguar. His successor, Jaguar Paw I, was the first of at least four rulers bearing variants of the same name, and is believed to be the ruler depicted on the Leiden Plate, a jadeite plaque with a date of AD 320, found in the nineteenth century on the Carribean coast, but attributed to Tikal. The tomb under Tikal's North Acropolis provisionally identified as Jaguar Paw I's was looted during the Late Classic period, destroying much evidence of his reign.

His descendant Jaguar Paw II, possibly a grandson, came to the throne some time before AD 376, and the two were formerly thought to be the same person. It is now clear that some four rulers came between them, in a confused period of rapid succession. Tikal's Stela 31 records Jaguar Paw II's death as being in AD 379.

The use of stelae (carved monoliths) to commemorate important events is largely a phenomenon of the Classic period in the Petén. Stelae are thus far more than just beautiful examples of Maya 'art' – they form a vital link in our knowledge of the Maya, and it is largely from the dates and other glyphs on stelae that the history of Tikal and other centres can be pieced together.

The successful decipherment of Maya glyphs is itself a recent phenomenon, and one which has revolutionized our understanding of the Maya. It had been thought that their society was peaceful and

Ball-court at Copán, in Honduras, with a small, square platform in the background similar to several at Tikal. Copán seems to have been the southernmost outpost of Tikal's sphere of influence. Three ball-courts have been found at Tikal, but only one very small example has been fully restored. The picture shows a fairly typical example of a fine Classic Maya court, with sloping sides, places for spectators to stand, and the stone ring through which players would seek to knock the rubber ball. The sacred ball-game seems to have been a major element of religious and social life in all Maya cities.

controlled by a priestly élite mostly concerned with religious observances. We now know that the Maya rulers were distinctly secular in their interests, and embarked on frequent wars in which their primary objectives were the capture and sacrifice of important opponents, and the enslavement of common soldiers.

These opening years of the Classic period saw the consolidation of Tikal as the dominant regional power. A stela at Uaxactún, dated AD 358 displays Tikal's emblem glyph, showing that Uaxactún had come under the control of its neighbour. The smaller centres nearby soon stopped erecting monuments at all, losing their identities under Tikal's growing might.

Tikal was not the only centre that had been consolidating its position. During this period Teotihuacán in the Valley of Mexico also emerged as an aggressive mercantile and military power. In the wake of the Ilopango disaster, Teotihuacán had established hegemony in the southern highlands as the region slowly became habitable again. The hybrid society of the highlands that developed under Teotihuacán influence, known as Esperanza, reached considerable heights of artistic and architectural achievement, and rebuilt the abandoned city of Kaminaljuyu.

The Teotihuacán-Kaminaljuyu axis apparently selected Tikal as its principal partner in the lowlands. The first evidence of this appears on Tikal's Stela 4, dated AD 378, which records the accession of the ruler Curl Nose. The style of this monument has distinctive Teotihuacán features: Curl Nose is depicted full face in a seated position, rather than in the usual Maya profile, standing upright.

When Curl Nose died after a 47-year reign, he was buried in a deep tomb under his funerary temple on the west face of the North Acropolis. His tomb and the offerings it contains − stucco-painted ceramics, animal offerings and an effigy of a southern god − bear a greater resemblance to those of Kaminaljuyu than to other tombs of Tikal, prompting speculation that Curl Nose himself was from Kaminaljuyu, perhaps attaining power by marriage into Tikal's ruling family.

The next but one ruler of Tikal was Stormy Sky, whose accession in AD 426 is commemorated in Stela 31, dated AD 435. In this monument Stormy Sky is depicted in profile in a return to Maya artistic traditions, but he is flanked by clearly Mexican warriors, identifiable by their

Left Fisherman's canoe shelter at sunset on Lake Petén Itzá. It seems that Tikal was once surrounded by similar lakes, but these are now dry and covered in jungle growth. Fish and water-fowl would have formed an important part of the diet at Tikal, which otherwise would have been poor in protein.

Left Glyphic inscriptions on the rear of Stela 31 in the Tikal Visitors' Centre. The inscriptions on this stela are by far the most important source for Tikal's history in the Early Classic period, despite the loss of some inscriptions from the base. The damage was caused when the stela was taken from its original position and built into the structure of Temple 33 in the North Acropolis after the death of Stormy Sky, the ruler commemorated on the stela's face.

Above right Modern Maya people loading a boat with sacks of maize and beans on Lake Atitlán in the Guatemalan highlands. The same foods were staples at Tikal, and were carried by cargo canoes through the jungle, along rivers and across lakes, to feed the city.

Below right Young Maya boy on his dug-out canoe on Lake Atitlán. Apart from the ubiquitous baseball hat, his head could equally well be shown on a painted pot in Tikal's museum.

weapons and the face of Tlaloc, the Mexican rain god, on a shield. At about the same time we see the introduction at Tikal of the Teotihuacán 'talud-tablero' architectural form, the projecting cornices on each step of a pyramid.

This was a time of rapid expansion for Tikal, whose emblem glyph is found on a wooden lintel radiocarbon-dated to AD 504 at Yaxchilán, some 100 miles to the west on the river Usumacinta, indicating a well-established presence by that time. Control of Yaxchilán, with its strategic location on a loop in the river, would have provided control over trade passing between the highlands and the Gulf coast. The artistic style then current in Tikal may also be seen at Yaxchilán, and as far afield as the south-eastern lowland centres of Copán and Quiriguá, providing signs of Tikal's growing sphere of influence.

The archaeological evidence of Early Classic burials confirms that Tikal was in a fast-expanding colonial phase. The wealthiest burials in this period are those of young male adults, indicating that the accumulation of personal wealth and prestige was possible for able men. This changes dramatically in Late Classic burials, where wealth is associated with the elderly. The social mobility this suggests would be expected in a time of rapid expansion and opportunity.

Many lowland centres may have been colonies established by Tikal, or perhaps were existing centres brought under its imperial wing, thus bringing strategic resources under its control. This period of expansion continued after Stormy Sky was laid to rest in Burial 48 under the North Acropolis in AD 456, and through the reigns of his successors Kan Boar, Bird Skull, and Jaguar Paw Skull 1st. After Jaguar Paw Skull the dynastic record becomes obscure, but there are indications that his wife, known as the Woman of Tikal, may herself have been one of perhaps four rulers of Tikal in quick succession following his death and prior to the accession of Double Bird, probably their son, in AD 537, as commemorated by Stela 17.

Tikal's magnificent Stela 17 marked the beginning of the Middle Classic hiatus, the period until roughly AD 593, which saw a dramatic decline in the erection of buildings and monuments throughout the Maya lowlands. This hiatus coincided with Teotihuacán's gradual decline in power, and its withdrawal from the Maya area. The hiatus was particularly marked in Tikal, which had formerly benefited from its special relationship with Teotihuacán.

Above Pyramid stairway at Tikal's Twin Pyramid Complex Q, on the path from the hotels to the Great Plaza. There are nine similar groups at Tikal, built to mark the passing of 20-year periods during the Late Classic era.

Below Detail of the terracing on Tikal's Pyramid of the Lost World. Architecturally, this echoes the *talud y tablero* style established at Teotihuacán in the Valley of Mexico, with stepped terracing and decorated vertical panels. The early influence of Teotihuacán on Tikal was an important factor in its rise to power.

In Tikal the hiatus seems to have lasted as late as AD 692, longer than at other lowland centres. Tikal continued as an urban centre during this time, but artistic and architectural output was negligible, and burials were accompanied by an impoverished collection of artefacts. Records of dynastic succession are broken and confused, the few surviving monuments deliberately having been defaced, indicating a time of political upheaval.

Although this period was one of decline for Tikal, it was to the benefit of the city's former colonies, which proclaimed growing independence through the use of their own emblem glyphs. In fact, Tikal's power may have started to wane before the hiatus. The earliest example of Yaxchilán's emblem glyph is on a monument dated AD 514, while Piedras Negras, another centre on the Usamacinta, uses its glyph on a lintel dated AD 534, just before Double Bird's rule began at Tikal. Copán's emblem glyph is first found on a stela dated AD 564. Palenque, a primary centre on the southern edge of the western lowlands, follows with a date of AD 602. Tikal by this time was well on the way to becoming one of many competing minor powers in the region.

In AD 682, Ah Cacau Caan Chac (also known as Moon Double

Iguana basking in the sunshine on old stones.

Comb), one of Tikal's greatest rulers, acceded to power. In some ways the new Tikal was to surpass its former glory, but no longer would it be the primary centre of the lowlands. From now on it would share its primacy with a handful of other centres: Copán in the south-east; Yaxchilán on the banks of the river Usumacinta; Palenque in the rich lands further west; and possibly Calakmul, an important Late Classic centre in the northern Petén which still awaits serious investigation.

Golden Age to Fall

Ah Cacau's accession took place exactly 13 katuns (cycles of 20 360-day years) after that of his revered predecessor Stormy Sky. In choosing this auspicious date, Tikal's élite was almost certainly trying to revive the greatness associated with Stormy Sky's reign after the long years of stagnation. Ah Cacau's family had already ruled Tikal for two generations, but neither his grandfather, nor his father Shield Skull had succeeded in reversing the decline. All hopes were vested in Ah Cacau, who represented the last chance for Tikal to regain its power and prestige.

During his reign of some 50 years, Ah Cacau succeeded in revitalizing Tikal's fortunes. Large new buildings were erected, public ceremonies revived and new alliances forged, for example with the nearby centre of Naranjo. A new structure was built over Stormy Sky's funerary temple to make it the largest building in the North Acropolis. This preserved the original building and its earlier additions. It also encased within its structure Stela 31, which records Tikal's early dynastic history. Ah Cacau also revived the practice of building twin pyramids to record katun endings, including Complex N to the west of the Great Plaza, with its portrait of the ruler on Stela 16.

Perhaps the most certain token of Tikal's return to greatness is Ah Cacau's magnificent funerary pyramid, Tikal's Temple 1, beneath which lies his spacious and lavishly endowed tomb, Burial 116. The splendid artefacts of jade, pearl, shell and ceramic that accompanied his journey to the underworld contrast handsomely with the impoverished offerings of the hiatus. Perhaps most interesting is a jade urn with a relief portrait on its lid, almost certainly of Ah Cacau. Carved bones in the tomb record military successes over Palenque, Copán and other centres. Burials of this period show wealth concentrated in the hands of mature adults rather than of younger men, as in the Preclassic era. This suggests that society was by now highly stratified, with little possibility of social advancement, and wealth concentrated in the hands of a distinct ruling class.

Ah Cacau's son Yax Kin Caan Chac (Night Sun Sky God), whose succession in AD 734 is recorded on Stela 21, was responsible for even greater building activity. For example Tikal's largest temple, Temple IV, in front of which Stela 21 was found, dates from this time. The temple door lintels (now in Basle, Switzerland) bear the date AD 741 along with Yax Kin's magnificently carved portrait. Temple IV's great roof-comb, the masonry tower at the apex of the structure, dated AD 766, bears extensive if severely eroded glyphic texts about Tikal's dynastic history.

The twin pyramids of Complex P in Tikal's North Zone were built to mark the end of the first katun (20-year period) of Yax Kin's reign, in AD 751, as recorded on Stela 20. The Temple of the Inscriptions and many of the wide ceremonial causeways that connect parts of the site may well also date from this time.

Yax Kin's tomb was first thought to be under Temple IV or Temple VI, but a more likely candidate had now emerged. This is Burial 196, a surprisingly rich tomb under a small structure south of Temple II in the Great Plaza. The offerings it contains bear many resemblances to those of Ah Cacau's tomb, especially the jade urn with a sculpted portrait on its lid, presumably representing Yax Kin. A carved bone from the tomb bears the date AD 766, two years before the accession of Dark Sun, thought to be Yax Kin's successor.

This seems to have been the time at which Tikal reached the peak of its greatness in terms of population and building activity, if not of territorial dominance. This carried on into the reign of Yax Kin's son, Chitam, whose accession in AD 766, about a year after his father's death, is recorded on Stela 22 in Complex Q. Chitam continued the tradition of building a twin pyramid group to mark the end of each katun. Those that he built, Group Q which commemorates AD 771, and Group R which commemorates AD 790, are the largest of the nine such groups built at Tikal.

While Chitam's burial has not been identified, Temple III, west of the Great Plaza, the last of Tikal's major Classic temples, is a strong possibility for his funerary temple. The wooden lintel in the shrine at its summit is finely carved with the image of a pot-bellied ruler, wrapped

Above Detail from a pot in the Tikal Museum showing a very fat merchant, apparently kneeling in obeisance to a ruler. Clearly, there was no shortage of food at Tikal for the entrepreneurial few.

Right Stela 5 under its thatched roof in Tikal's Great Plaza. The stela is heavily eroded in places, and incomplete, having been damaged during early investigations. Nonetheless, it is a superb example of Maya carving, and shows the Late Classic ruler, Yax Kin, with an ornate feather head-dress and other accoutrements of office. It has been dated to AD 744.

in a jaguar skin and flanked by obsequious attendants. This well-preserved carving must represent either Chitam, or less probably, an unknown subsequent ruler.

After Chitam, or perhaps even during his reign, Tikal entered into a second and final period of decline in its power and prosperity. No building has been identified any later than AD 830, a date which passed uncommemorated anywhere in the Maya lowlands, perhaps due to dire predictions associated with that date. By the time of Tikal's latest known monuments, Altar 11 and the accompanying Stela 11, dated AD 869, that decline had become irreversible.

The fine ceramics known as Imix, associated with the Late Classic era at Tikal, had disappeared, to be replaced with a degenerate variant known as Eznab. The distribution of Eznab potsherds shows that the population of Tikal had fallen in the space of a few decades from a peak of some 45,000 or more to a mere 3-4,000. The quality of craftsmanship and the undignified accumulations of rubbish show us that those who remained were living like squatters in abandoned palaces, and looting the tombs of long-dead rulers. By roughly the end of the tenth century Tikal had been completely abandoned.

This was not an isolated phenomenon. Similar events, examined in more detail in Chapter 4, were taking place throughout the region, affecting primary centres throughout the lowlands, and to a lesser extent the whole Maya area. This was more than another hiatus, more than just the fall of Tikal. It was the collapse of Mesoamerica's most advanced indigenous civilization.

City in the Jungle

The evidence of the Classic Maya monuments and writings is of dynastic history and culture. But it tells nothing of how Maya society was sustained, nor about its evolving relationship with the environment. Environmental factors have always been vital in shaping the destiny of peoples, and Tikal is no exception.

From the earliest days, Mayanists found it hard to recognize the jungle-shrouded ruins of Mayan cities as the product of an advanced indigenous civilization. Early explorers invented a bewildering range of theories to explain their origin, based on anything from Atlantean mythology to the wanderings of lost tribes of Israel. They simply could not believe that civilization could flourish in an environment apparently

Above Two long and narrow buildings on the west side of Court 6 in the Central Acropolis, which was probably used to house Tikal's religious hierarchy. The Acropolis was an absolute warren of stairways, courts, hidden chambers and interlocking palaces, and has only been partly restored.

Below The southern row of temples of the North Acropolis, deserted by late afternoon, with the majority of visitors already halfway back to comfortable hotels in Guatemala City. Temple 22 in the background is now the highest structure in the Acropolis, and catches the last rays of the setting sun.

so hostile to human endeavour. The rainforest represented nature at its most alarming: the dark tangle of forest, alternately swampy then drought-stricken, the hazards of poisonous snakes, biting insects, dangerous diseases, and the echo of threatening roars. Any civilization existing here was assumed to have its origins in more temperate climes, and to have been inherently doomed.

This view was largely due to European prejudice, unable to accept that the ancestors of 'savages' could have attained such heights. Yet the modern Maya peoples themselves, as they worship ancient gods in the ruins, find it easier to take refuge in the supernatural than to confront the reality that the builders of the temples were their own ancestors.

A modern analysis of the rainforest environment leads to different conclusions. The builders of Tikal had been there for some 5,000 years, long enough to adapt successfully. As with indigenous peoples around the world, they were skilled in the use of available resources. They had developed a knowledge of the jungle's products: edible fruits, nuts, leaves and roots; medicinal plants; and the game that flourished there, deer, armadillo, monkey and tapir, to name a few. And they had developed a range of productive agricultural systems.

Rainforest soils are generally held to be infertile and nutrient poor, but in fact there is enormous variation in the quality of such soils. Recent analysis of soils around Tikal has shown that their quality is unusually good. Up to 86 per cent of soils in the central 100 square miles around Tikal are of high fertility, as opposed to 37 per cent in the whole central lowlands. This alone explains the location of Tikal. Populations would naturally concentrate in areas of high soil fertility, and combine their efforts in defence, temple building and the performance of rituals, and other aspects of community organization. From such humble origins, centres like Tikal grew over the centuries.

Other factors favouring Tikal's location are less obvious. Building stone was plentiful, but no more than elsewhere in the Petén. The Tikal region is poor in some other resources, such as salt, hard volcanic stone for tools such as the stones used to grind maize into dough, and obsidian, the black volcanic glass used for knives and tools. Although obsidian was imported, the locally abundant flint was at least an adequate substitute, and undoubtedly important in the early days.

Tikal is surprisingly remote from rivers and other types of trade route for a city so dependent on imported resources. On the other hand, it stands on a land bridge connecting navigable rivers to east and west, and if the low-lying bajos (now seasonal swamps) around Tikal were once lakes, as has been suggested, these would have further increased the distance over which goods could be carried by boat. In any case, the population of Tikal was mostly self-sufficient in basic necessities, and the city's remoteness would have been a strong defensive asset.

Water was the single most critical resource in sustaining life at Tikal. As one Spanish chronicler wrote:

> Nature worked so differently in this country in the matter of rivers and springs, which in all the rest of the world run on top of land, that here in this country all run and flow through secret passages under it.

The importance of water is underlined by the importance of the rain god Chac in the Maya pantheon. This is not because of any real shortage of rain – Tikal enjoys roughly 50 inches of rain a year, lying midway between the wetter Maya highlands, and the dryer Yucatán. However, this entirely adequate rainfall is concentrated in the May-November rainy season, with near-drought occurring at other times. The rainwater rapidly flows down to the water table, which a restored well near Tikal shows to be as low as 500 feet.

The problem of this annual drought was the central challenge to be overcome by the people of Tikal. Twelve large reservoirs have been found, with a combined capacity of many million gallons of water, more than enough for domestic use, but inadequate to irrigate crops. If the bajos near Tikal were originally lakes, they would have provided valuable water storage for irrigation, as well as allowing water-borne trade. Images incised on bones found in a burial in Tikal's Temple 1, now enlarged into murals at the site museum, show aquatic scenes with canoe-borne gods and fishermen. It seems likely that these depict the bajos during the Classic period. This theory is supported by the discovery of earthworks around Tikal's perimeter, which would have combined with the lakes to form a complete defensive barrier.

Feeding the Multitude

Even if the bajos were lakes, thus ensuring Tikal's water supply, much work remains to explain how the population was fed. Until recently, it

View from the narrow platform around the base of Temple IV's roof-comb, facing east towards the Great Plaza. Temples I and II are on the left, with the rear of Temple III in the centre. The tip of Temple V's roof-comb can just be seen over the great tree-covered mass of the South Acropolis. Over to the right is the Lost World Pyramid.

Rear view of Temple 1's roof-comb, taken from the eastern end of the Central Acropolis. The building mounds in the foreground, which have only been partly cleared, give an idea of what the whole site was like before excavation and restoration.

Detail of the stairway to Temple 32 in the North Acropolis.

was assumed that the only agricultural system in use among the Maya was 'slash and burn', whereby they cut and burnt the vegetation, and planted the cleared land with maize, squash and beans for a year or two, then allowing the soil to lie fallow for several years before clearing and planting it again. It is now clear that while slash and burn was important, especially in outlying areas, the Maya had other, more sophisticated methods.

The figures speak for themselves. Tikal's centre covered an area of some 25 square miles with an estimated population of 39,000 people. Another 6,000 lived in the less densely settled outer 25 square miles, giving a total population of some 45,000 with an average density of 950 per square mile. Under the reigns of Ah Cacau and Yax Kin, the population was even higher, and figures up to 70,000 have been proposed. This is well short of what is generally defined as 'urban' – around 5,000 per square mile – but equally far in excess of what can be supported by slash and burn. On a slash-and-burn rotation of one year's cultivation in five, 1 square mile at Tikal has been shown capable of supporting no more than 150 people, one-sixth of the actual figure.

A number of theories have been proposed to explain this enormous discrepancy. Fish and water fowl from the bajos would have provided valuable protein. Root crops, such as sweet potato, yam and manioc, were important staples supplementing maize. These yield about double the calories of maize from a given area, and can grow on relatively poor soil. This would have been useful, since maize rapidly depletes the nutrients even of fertile soils. Thus the Maya may have grown maize and root crops alternately on the same land, perhaps in rotation with fallow periods or crops such as tomato, beans, gourds and chili. It is also likely that they used fertilizers, in the form of wood ash and animal and human manure.

We can also be certain that the Maya harvested forest tree crops. Attention has focused on the ramón (breadnut) tree, which produces large protein-rich nuts. These trees are still found concentrated around sites, indicating that they were deliberately cultivated. Also associated with ramón trees are high concentrations of 'chultunes', artificial caverns dug into the bedrock. While the purpose of chultunes remains unproven, it has been convincingly argued that some at least were storage pits for ramón nuts, capable of keeping them fresh for months.

The attention given to ramón trees has drawn the focus away from other important trees associated with archaeological sites, such as papaya, avocado, zapote and mamey, which all yield nutritious fruit. It is possible that such trees may have been planted in orchards, or even in an artificial forest environment, together with other desirable plants, thus allowing intensive year round production.

There are signs in the lowland Maya region of other advanced agricultural practices. Remains of raised field systems for intensive agriculture have been found in bajos and along riverbanks, although it is hard to estimate their former extent. Large areas of terracing have been found in the Maya mountains to the west of Tikal, in the Río Bec region to the north, and in the southern ridge lands just 20 miles to the south-east. Such terraces would have improved crop yields and soil conservation, but there is no evidence that they were used in the immediate area of Tikal.

Clearly, the inhabitants of Tikal would have imported some food, and paid for it by exports of other goods. Although they had carried on an active trade in manufactured goods such as textiles and ceramics, the basis of Tikal's economy and the principal occupation of its people was agriculture. Key items such as salt, of which as much as 50 tonnes a year was needed, were carried in by porters, but it does not seem likely that food for the labouring classes was imported in significant quantities, given the limitations on transportation.

Further research and experimentation is needed to verify these theories, and would perhaps yield models of productive rainforest agriculture in the process, of great relevance today. But taken together, the different techniques described would go a long way to explain the delicate balance with the environment that enabled the people of Tikal to feed themselves.

2   The Classic Maya

Pyramids and Palaces

After the fall of Tikal and the other Classic centres, the Maya people and culture would live on, but the heights of Classic Maya civilization were not again equalled. This chapter examines that civilization and its achievements, concentrating especially on architecture, the most enduring and most impressive of Maya artistic expressions, and fundamental to the Maya world order. The main forms and elements of Maya architecture are simply expressed, with just three primary building types – temple pyramids, palaces, and ball-courts – which remained constant throughout the distinct and evolving styles of different periods and geographical areas.

One or more groups of temple pyramids formed the focus of Maya ceremonial centres, and they usually stood on a raised platform known as an acropolis. Unlike the pyramids of Egypt, these have stepped terraces and a ceremonial stairway leading up to a platform, with a stone temple chamber at the summit in most cases. The relative proportions of the different elements vary enormously. At Tikal for instance, the main pyramids are tall and steep, with small temple chambers; elsewhere, the proportions are reversed. The exact purpose and use of these structures are not known, but clearly they served for worship, for the burial of noble dead, and in some places for astronomical observation.

Many temples, most notably at Tikal, also support massive roof combs, an innovation of the Classic Maya. This weight requires a great mass of supporting masonry, in some cases reducing the width of the chambers below to just a few feet. This is the case at Tikal, where temples are very constricted but have roof-combs rising vertically from the rear wall to an impressive height, generally greater than that of the temple itself. We know that the roof-combs at Tikal were highly ornamented with sculpture and painting. However, little has survived of the decorations, which have been directly exposed to the elements for over a millenium.

By comparison to Tikal, Palenque's Temple of the Cross has about six times the floor area for masonry walls of the same width, a far lighter roof that follows the line of the arches beneath, and a lightweight roof-comb placed above the central divide, reaching up a mere 8 feet or so. Thus while at Palenque space was an important consideration, at Tikal the emphasis was on grandeur at the expense of interior space.

Side view of Temple I's soaring roof-comb, which together with its supporting chamber forms one third of the temple's overall height of 145 feet. The comb was built in two sections with a hollow, sealed chamber in each to reduce its weight. Such massive roof-combs are a distinctive feature of Classic Maya architecture in the Petén.

The second main building type is the palace, long rectangular buildings of narrow chambers, again often on raised platforms. These were probably used as residences by members of the priestly nobility and rulers, although in some cases it is not clear whether a particular building served as a temple or a palace. The third type is the ball-court, a rectangular space with sloping walls for playing the sacred ball game; the game was played by two teams, each trying to knock a hard rubber ball through a stone hoop, using only hips and elbows. Ball-courts are found in most Maya sites.

At Tikal and other lowland Maya sites, the tall stone tablet known as a stela was a fourth architectural element of considerable importance. They are invariably found in large numbers around the ceremonial centres, and are associated with round 'altars' placed at their feet. Some are ornately carved, with complex date glyphs and portraits of rulers. Beautiful though the stelae may be, this was secondary to their apparent main purpose, to create an enduring record of major historical events and to maintain the prestige of ruling dynasties. There is little doubt that stelae had a ritual or religious significance also, perhaps in ancestor worship. One unfortunate aspect of this is that the Maya would 'sacrifice' or deface stelae to assert the dominance of one dynastic faction over another. There are many examples of disfigured stelae at Tikal and elsewhere.

In spite of this, a great number of stelae have survived; it is from them that we are able to recreate the history of the Classic Maya. While the stela cult was clearly advanced at Tikal, it reached its peak in Quiriguá, which has the tallest stela in the Maya area, the 36-foot Stela E, and at nearby Copán, where the quality of carving on its 12-foot stelae is without parallel in the Maya world.

The basis of Tikal's lowland Maya architecture was established in the Preclassic period, at sites such as El Mirador. Limestone causeways or 'sacbeob' were also in use at El Mirador, connecting different parts of the site, and these are features in most Classic sites, including Tikal. Several important architectural changes marked the onset of the Classic period. Up until this time, the temple chambers on pyramids were either temporary structures of wood and palm fronds, or had masonry walls supporting a temporary roof. However, the Classic period saw the construction of corbelled stone roofs, originally in tomb vaults, but later in other buildings such as temples and palaces.

Above Palace on the main plaza at Copán. Although directly contemporaneous with Tikal, the architectural style is distinct. It lacks the great pyramid temples and palaces. Instead, the emphasis is on creating harmonious spaces, which unite sculpture and architecture.

Below left Head of a vulture adorning the façade of a palace at Copán.

Below right Fish motif on the geometrically ornamented cornice of the palace at Copán illustrated above.

Overleaf A visitor laboriously making his way up the steep (60°) Magician's Pyramid at Uxmal in Mexico – the descent will be tougher still. It is hard to imagine how the Maya priests and rulers could have climbed the pyramids in full regalia while retaining the necessary dignity for ceremonial occasions.

Thus a kind of arch was developed (though not the true arch), in which the weight of stone above is resolved along the line of the arch. The Maya arch is built of successive horizontal layers of stone creeping inwards from both sides over a gap to be bridged, until they meet in the centre. It is interesting to speculate on the soaring masterpieces of stone that the Maya might have constructed had they discovered the true arch, but, despite the wide variety of shapes of corbelled arch, this was not to be. Masterpieces they did construct, but within the limitations imposed by their technology.

The key limitation on their buildings was the size of gap that could be bridged by the corbelled arch, no more than 10 feet, and usually less than half that distance. Another limitation was the huge weight of masonry involved in building the arch, which in turn required massive walls to support it. It was also difficult for the Maya to construct multi-storey buildings, and they did not attempt this until the Late Classic period. On the other hand, the Maya arch provided a remarkable degree of resistance to earthquake damage, a danger in parts of the Maya area.

The Classic Yucatán Styles

Three variations on the Classic style are of particular importance, all developing in the Yucatán peninsula in the late Classic and early Postclassic eras. In Río Bec, the vertical theme is carried to the extreme, the pyramid evolving into a tower of solid masonry, in which the steps and staircase are reduced to mere decorative elements, topped with an inaccessible temple complete with roof-comb. These towers form the corners of a temple enclosure, in which the ceremonies no longer conducted on the pyramids presumably took place.

Broadly contemporaneous with Río Bec is the Puuc style. Puuc is best known for elegant palace façades, decorated with stone and stucco masks. The thin facing of intricately sculpted limestone over a rubble core is often modelled into a geometric mosaic, or occasionally into animal and human forms. Columns, unknown in the Petén, are used to create spacious interiors. Pyramid temples are rare, and generally less steep than in the Petén, with a series of intermediate platforms. Stelae are also uncommon, and clearly had a lesser religious significance than

Above The Palace of the Governor at Uxmal, in the Yucatán peninsula. This was the last of the great buildings constructed at the site, and it is a superb example of the late 'Puuc' style of architecture. The palace is 330 feet long, in three sections, and was probably used as residential quarters for Uxmal's ruling family. The mosaic cornice consists of tens of thousands of separately carved limestone pieces, forming an intricate geometric design, interposed with rain god masks and serpent motifs. The absolute mastery of the masons is shown by the fact that the walls slope slightly out from the vertical to correct the natural visual distortion of an eye-level perspective. The ancient Greeks were also aware of this secret.

Below The main plaza at Quiriguá, a small site some 30 miles up the fertile Motagua river valley from Copán. Now surrounded by thousands of acres of Del Monte banana plantations, Quiriguá is best known for its remarkable Classic-period carved stelae and monuments.

in the Petén. The most famous Puuc centre is Uxmal in the northern Yucatán, one of the peninsula's most visited sites.

The Chenes region, between Puuc and Río Bec in the central Yucatán, contains distinctive variants on the architectural themes of its neighbours. The Chenes style develops the ornamentation of the Puuc to a baroque extreme. These three styles were followed by the more Mexicanized Maya Toltec style, typified by Chichén Itzá in the Yucatán. This style has been characterized as militaristic and stark, not least because scholars have tended to deride the architecture of the Postclassic as compared to the Classic. This derision is quite unjustified, as a high architectural standard was achieved, notably in the Early Postclassic period, with a range of distinctive and original styles.

The Plastic Arts

With all the Maya styles, the carving of wood and stone was a key part of architectural decoration. At Tikal, the stelae are the best example of stone carving, and there are few remaining examples of other decorative stone carving. Nearly as durable as stone is the lime stucco widely used both for interior and exterior decoration. This was made from crushed limestone, burnt to quicklime. When mixed with water, it solidified into a hard and long-lasting material which was used as we use concrete, mortar or plaster. Many stucco masks at Tikal have been preserved, decorating the exterior of pyramids, while the stucco facing of many interior walls has also survived.

We are fortunate in the remarkable durability of sapodilla wood, used by the craftsmen of Tikal for the carved lintels of doors between temple chambers on the great pyramids. Sapodilla lintels and the carvings they bear are often better preserved than stone in a comparable situation. Smaller items of carved wood have not fared so well, and few have been found.

Smaller pieces of precious and semi-precious stone such as jadeite are more frequent finds, principally in burials and associated caches. These show considerable skill in their making, especially as jadeite is exceptionally hard and the craftsmen had no metal tools. Sometimes fuchsite, a softer stone which resembles jadeite, was used instead. Figurines and heads were popular items, as were plaques such as the Leiden Plate, mentioned earlier in this chapter. Some superb examples of chipped flint sceptres and other ceremonial items also exist from the

Vaulted passage under a palace at Copán. The stepped stonework clearly illustrates the principle of the Maya or corbelled arch, in which the mass of stone above makes each half of the arch self-supporting. This technique gave enormous strength against earthquakes, but limited the possible achievement of Maya masons.

Classic period, which display absolute mastery of this hard, brittle material.

Ceramic material also survives well, although it is only the ceremonial items placed in the tombs of the great that are usually found intact. But to the archaeologist this is often not important. The nature of an original article is easily deduced from fragments by a trained eye, making potsherds a rich source of information. Due to the changing nature of the pots in use, comparison of the potsherds on different parts of a site allows the archaeologist to see which parts were in contemporaneous use. In the same way, potsherds found within a building structure help to date its construction. Similarities between potsherds found on different sites are vital evidence of trading links between them.

The Maya created a bewildering variety of ceramic forms for utilitarian and ceremonial purposes, but the most admired is the decorated polychrome pottery of the Late Classic era, with black and red painted designs on a cream, cinnamon or orange base. Despite the finer decoration of the Late Classic ceramics, the quality of firing is in many cases inferior. While the production of ceramics began as a domestic affair, there is evidence that the Late Classic Maya were using moulds to mass-produce ceramics in specialized factories, and continued to do so into the Postclassic period.

Little Classic Maya painting has survived, but from what remains, it is clear that they were accomplished artists, using a wide palette of colours. Vegetable-based pigments have oxidized away, and only mineral- and charcoal-based colours have survived. Decorations were painted on to a wide variety of surfaces: ceramics, sculptures of stone and stucco, and lime plastered walls. Stelae, for example, often bear traces of red hematite, indicating that these were painted rather than kept as bare stone. It seems that even temples and palaces may have been painted in their entirety.

The single outstanding example of painting from the Classic Maya lowlands is at Bonampak, a small centre in the Usumacinta region near Yaxchilán. The paintings here, tentatively dated at AD 790, completely cover the interior of three rooms. They are exceptional for their natural style, excellent state of preservation, and the unique insight they provide into the life of the Late Classic Maya. They depict firstly the preparations for warfare, the ruler consulting with generals; the

Above Group of Late Classic temples at Palenque, in Mexico, rising from artificial mounds that were once terraced and stuccoed. The roof-combs are far smaller than the contemporaneous examples at Tikal, and are pierced to reduce their weight. As a result, the weight of supporting masonry is considerably reduced, and the interior spaces of the temple chambers are correspondingly larger.

Below Small square platform in the main plaza of Copán, perhaps used as the focus of ceremonies, or for performances.

sequence moves to the ensuing battle, in which Bonampak was victorious and took many prisoners; finally we see the celebrations which followed, and the gruesome torture of prisoners. Most other surviving Maya paintings are from the Postclassic era, to the north in the Yucatán; the war-like paintings in Chichén Itzá's Temple of the Warriors and Temple of the Jaguars are good examples. Rare examples of Preclassic mural painting survive at Tikal, in burials beneath the North Acropolis.

Knowledge is limited by the perishability of most media, only the most durable materials surviving a millenium in the jungle. We can only guess at the textiles used by the Maya of Tikal, for example – though textiles woven by today's Maya contain elements that may be recognized from Classic carvings. Information about basketwork and the use of feathers in personal ornamentation is similarly scarce, although carvings show that both were important. Multi-coloured feathers such as the plumes of the sacred quetzal bird were exported in large quantities from the Maya area, and these served as a kind of currency, along with seashells and cocoa beans.

The Science of Time

The Maya obsession with time generated one of the supreme intellectual achievements of the New World: the complex, interlocking calendrical systems of the Classic period. Their complexity reflected an esoteric importance in divination and a significance far greater than that of a simple device for marking the passage of time.

The Maya used three calendars, the Long Count, the 'vague year', and the sacred almanac, each serving a different purpose. In the Long Count calendar, which they used for the long-term measurement of time, dates are taken from a starting date of 0.0.0.0.0 in 3114 BC. The calender is based on a 360-day year (tun) comprised of 18 months (uinals) of 20 days (kins) each. Each cycle of 20 years makes a katun, and each cycle of 20 katuns makes a baktun, a period of 144,000 days; 13 baktuns completes the great cycle, returning to 0.0.0.0.0. All Long Count dates are expressed as a series of five numbers; for example, AD 1991 would be 12.18.18.0.0. From right to left, the first number represents kins, the second uinals, the third tuns, the fourth katuns, and the fifth baktuns.

Using the Long Count, an error with respect to the approximately 365-day solar cycle will arise, reaching about 1 full year in 70. Thus there was a separate, concurrent year, known as the 'haab' or 'vague year', of 365 days, composed of 18 20-day months (uinals), and a single unlucky month of 5 days at the end.

The 365-day year was still not completely accurate, though better than the calender in use in Europe at the same time. But the Maya were certainly aware of the discrepancy, which we account for with our leap years, and may well have taken corrective steps of which we are unaware. The problem was not one of observation, but of how to reconcile the various cycles without upsetting the delicate balance.

In addition, they used a 260-day sacred almanac, which dictated the timing of ceremonies and was crucial in divination. This year was not divided into months, but combined a repeating series of twenty day names with a concurrent sequence of numbers running up to 13. Thus the almanac cycle works through 260 different combinations of day names and numbers before repeating itself.

The next level of complexity is the interlocking of the 365-day vague year and the 260-day sacred almanac. Any day was defined in terms of both systems. Like two interlocking cogs, one of 365 teeth and the other of 260, any given position of the two cogs only returns after 73 revolutions of the smaller and 52 of the larger. Thus 52 vague years or 73 sacred almanacs make a further unit of 18,980 days, known as the calendar round.

Of these systems, all were common across Mesoamerica save the Long Count, a uniquely Maya invention originating in the late Preclassic period. The dates on stelae include information from all three calendars, and more besides. The Long Count date is usually followed by the sacred almanac date, the name glyph of an associated deity, an additional glyph which is not understood, a sequence of five glyphs apparently describing the lunar and planetary situation, and a final glyph expressing the date in the 365-day vague year.

Astronomy was an exact science for the Maya. We have evidence from Copán that 149 lunar cycles had been measured as lasting 4,400 days, an error of just 7 minutes over a year. Venus was another important feature of the Maya cosmology. We know from the Dresden Codex (one of the Maya writings which escaped de Landa's bonfire) that the period of Venus' movement round the sun was known to

Left East side of the Magician's Pyramid at Uxmal in the Yucatán peninsula, said to have been built in one night by the magician in question. The name Uxmal means 'thrice built', but in fact this unique oval-plan temple was rebuilt five times between the sixth and eleventh centuries before the site was finally abandoned, apparently due to lack of water.

Below right Seated person, presumably of a certain importance, gesturing dismissively at an applicant. Detail from a polychrome vase, found in Burial 116 under Tikal's Temple 1, now in the site museum.

Below far right A fragment of stone carving, found in a hidden chamber in Tikal's North Acropolis. Known as Stela 32, in fact it is almost certainly not part of a stela. The figure depicted is thought to be the Mexican rain god, Tlaloc. The style of the carving shows an influence from Teotihuacán in the Valley of Mexico, and demonstrates the close links that existed between Teotihuacán and Tikal in the Early Classic period.

Right The magnificently baroque Monument 16 at Quiriguá (also known as Zoomorph P), dated to AD 795. Early archaeologists christened it the 'Great Turtle Altar', although it is doubtful that is was ever used as an altar. The monument is about 9 feet long, and the focus of its design is a ruler of Quiriguá seated in the jaws of a great turtle, or possibly a jaguar. The rest of the surface is completely decorated with relief carvings of humans, masks, animals, symbols and glyphic inscriptions.

within an accuracy of 2 hours over its 584-day cycle. They were even aware that there was a slight error, and occasional corrections were inserted into the Venus calendar.

There is evidence that the Maya were also aware of the movements of other planets visible to the naked eye; one Classic glyph has been interpreted as a reference to Saturn. The Pole Star, around which the skies apparently revolve, was also important in the Maya cosmology, and provided a direction for the alignment of many Maya structures. Accurate observations of this sort are not difficult where there are good lines of sight and suitable horizon markers to provide a basis of comparison. The Incas of the Andes and the prehistoric peoples of Europe were also well aware of this. The peaks of Maya pyramids would have provided ideal sighting points, and some centres were clearly designed with astronomy in mind.

One example is at Uaxactún, 25 miles north of Tikal, where the arrangement of the pyramids allows accurate determination of solstices and equinoxes (the shortest and longest days, and the two days of equal day and night), from the position of the sunrise. There are certainly many other such observatories awaiting discovery.

Underlying these intellectual achievements is the numerical system of the Classic Maya. It was based on a system in common with other Mesoamerican peoples: the writing of numbers as a combination of bars (value five) and dots (value one). However, the Maya took this to a new level by combining it with a system based on the number 20, as opposed to our own based on 10. Significantly, this required the use of the zero, represented by a stylized shell. The Maya were thus one of a very few civilizations in the world who arrived at the concept of zero, unknown to the ancient Romans and Greeks, but so vital to all areas of advanced mathematics.

Maya Writing

The knowledge of Maya society was recorded and preserved in codices (painted manuscripts), treasured and passed from one generation of priests to the next. Many of these survived the Spanish Conquest, but as Bishop Diego de Landa wrote in his 1562 *Relación de las cosas del Yucatán:*

Above left Stela in the main plaza at Copán, carved in fine-textured andesite from a nearby quarry. Traces of red paint can be seen on this and other stelae at Copán, but lichens and algae also add a range of colours. The stela has obviously been broken and reassembled, and the face of the figure has been lost. The glyphic inscriptions up the side have been well preserved, and give details of dates, astrology and genealogical events.

Below left Detail of a realistically carved face from a stela in the great plaza of Copán. Fortunately, the Tikal custom of defacing stelae after the death of the ruler depicted does not seem to have been current at Copán, and thus these masterpieces are preserved.

Above right Stylized head of a warrior at Copán, wearing large earplugs, awaiting reinstatement in its original position on the decorated cornice of a palace.

Below right Larger than life-size head at Copán that was probably part of a temple cornice decoration, but is now detached and also awaiting eventual reinstatement. It is undoubtedly a true portrait, showing a slightly bad-tempered, middle-aged man, apparently in need of dental attention.

We found a large number of books in these characters and, as they contained nothing in which there was to be seen superstition and lies of the devil, we burned them all, which they regretted to an amazing degree.

Most of the information presented in this chapter has been painstakingly deciphered from Maya writings, carved on stone or painted onto walls, ceramics and the few codices that escaped burning. Even now, although researchers have grasped the principles in operation, there is still much that remains to be understood. Certainly, the Maya writing system was the most sophisticated in the Americas.

In appearance, Maya writing consists of arrays of approximate squares with rounded corners, each containing a number of symbols. Each such square is known as a glyph group, while the individual symbols within each group are known as glyphs. Typically a group will contain a central main glyph, and a choice of one or more sub-glyphs, above, below, or to each side of the main glyph. Around 800 glyphs have now been deciphered, and new additions are constantly being made. The process has been very confusing, since evidence is scarce and there is no single unifying principle behind the writings. Some glyphs are representational, while others denote spoken syllables, although this may depend on the context, or on the Maya language in question.

Much decipherment has been based on the so-called de Landa alphabet, compiled by Bishop de Landa in order to allow translation of biblical texts into Maya languages. Unfortunately he did not understand their writing system so, for example, the letter 'h' in the Maya alphabet is translated as the syllable sounding like 'aitch', rather than the actual sound of that letter in speech. This has been the cause of much misunderstanding over the last century or so of Maya scholarship.

It is one of the ironies of history that we are so much indebted to the book-burning Bishop de Landa, not only for his alphabet, but for a huge amount of other information about the Maya civilization found by the conquistadors. For all his prejudices, de Landa's writings are the best we have. Yet it was de Landa who was responsible for the burning of hundreds of Maya volumes at Maní in July 1562, an act of intellectual vandalism comparable with the burning of the Great Library of Alexandria. With just three exceptions now in European

Part of the East court at Copán, still under restoration, a painstaking process similar to reassembling a giant jigsaw puzzle. Large sections of the buildings around the court have fallen into the river below, eaten away by seasonal floods.

museums, those volumes that survived the burning have almost certainly succumbed to the ravages of time.

The volumes burnt at Maní were not originals from the Classic period, although it is perfectly conceivable that they may have been copies, or copies of copies, from the Classic. It is certain that the Classic Maya had books, as disintegrating fragments have been discovered in Classic tombs at several sites in the Maya area including Uaxactún. Another late codex from El Mirador in Chiapas, Mexico (not the major Preclassic centre) is kept in the Mexican National Museum of Anthropology awaiting restoration – the bark-based paper has decayed but its lime coating has survived along with the writings.

While nothing is known of Classic Maya codices, speculation is possible on the basis of the later codices which survived. These are the Dresden and Madrid Codices, which are about astronomy and divination, and the Paris Codex, which deals with rituals, gods and astrology, and included indications of a Maya zodiac comparable to our own, with thirteen animal signs. While this suggests that the dominant concerns of Maya literature were religious, we will never know what range of subjects were covered.

Religion and Society

Much of our information about later Maya religion and ideology comes from de Landa, who recorded his observations of the customs and observances of the Yucatán Maya. Further insights are gained from the codices described above. While it is difficult to extrapolate reliably the 700 years back to the Classic period, especially as considerable Mexican influence had reached the Maya area, we can assume continuity in most areas.

The basic focus of Maya religion was to engage the assistance of supernatural forces in achieving earthly objectives such as health, long life, and good harvests. For the Maya, the visible and invisible worlds were indistinguishable, and all visible forms, such as trees, mountains, rivers and animals, were endowed with invisible powers. The rituals and observances of the Maya were intended to propitiate the numerous gods of their pantheon, and to ensure the harmonious unfolding of time.

Mind-altering substances were used by the priesthood to bring the

Above The circular Observatory building in the older part of Chichén Itzá to the south of the site. The inner part may have been built by Maya peoples before the arrival of Toltec influence in Postclassic times. Unlike most buildings at Maya sites, the name in current use is known to be accurate. The conquistadors who found the site christened the Observatory 'El Caracol' (The Snail). Within the tower, a spiral stair leads up to a chamber which gives sight-lines for the astronomical and solar observation that was so important for the Maya religion and calendar.

Below The east court at Palenque, seen from the tower in the Palace complex. On either side of the stairway in the court are bas-relief stone panels, showing nine individuals in an unusually naturalistic style. The scene is one of judgement, with the naked figure on the right apparently the offender, and the eight others involved in passing sentence. The carvings were moved here in the Late Classic era, but seem to date from an earlier time.

Left Detail of the façade from the House of the Turtles, at Uxmal, one of the minor gems of Maya architecture. Above the simple decoration of the cornice are the turtles for which the building is named, each one slighly different.

Below left Bas-relief panel on a temple at Yaxchilán, 60 miles west of Tikal on the Usumacinta river. A player of the sacred ball-game is shown, fallen to one knee.

Below right Detail of a mosaic cornice decoration on the west building of the Nunnery Quadrangle at Uxmal. The stone-mason has boldly over-laid the conventionally static geometric design with a dynamic serpent motif, apparently weaving in and out of the stonework.

Right The main archway into the Nunnery Quadrangle, passing through the relatively undecorated building on the southern side. As a general rule, the plainer buildings are older – the Puuc style became more embellished in later years.

Below left Detail of glyphic inscriptions from a well-preserved Classic period stela, found at the minor site of Ixtutz in the Petén, but now in the Guatemala City Archaeological Museum.

Below right Temple of the Foliated Cross at Palenque. The façade has fallen away, revealing the construction technique and demonstrating the strength of the corbelled arch.

ordinarily unseen world into view. Hallucinogenic mushrooms, herbal preparations, cigars of wild tobacco and other leaves, and perhaps the poison of the tropical toad, were apparently used to bring about altered states of consciousness. But most commonly used, at least by the common people, was undoubtedly alcohol fermented from maize, agave cactus and honey. According to early observers, all rituals and festivals ended with long bouts of drunkenness, a tradition that survives in Maya villages to this day.

There is no reason to believe that religion was connected with a code of ethics such as that of Christianity. The orientation was rather towards a complex esoteric knowledge, the successful manipulation of which would help to bring about desired objectives; another purpose of this knowledge was divination. As we have already seen, the calendar was vital for divination, and the maintenance of the calendar was one of many priestly functions.

Maya religion was polytheistic, indeed the number of gods and lesser deities is so large as to be bewildering. Every aspect of life had its presiding deity, as had every unit of time within each of the different calendrical systems. And each deity needed to be honoured at the right time and in the correct manner. Each number from 0-13 also had its own deity, and these numbers are sometimes represented by a deity glyph rather than by the numerical system.

The principal gods depicted in the codices include Itzamna, the creator god and lord of the heavens, who also manifests as the sun god; Chac, the benevolent rain god, associated with life-giving forces; Yum Kaax, the god of maize and agriculture, whose head-dress is shaped like an ear of maize; Yum Cimil, the skeletal death god, who is feared among the Maya to this day; and Buluc Chabtan, the god of warfare, violence and human sacrifice, who may be based on a Toltec god.

A simplified version of this polytheism has survived to this day in the conversion of the Maya to Catholicism, whereby the saints and the Holy Trinity became equated with the old gods. A further factor which facilitated Maya acceptance of Christianity was the sanctity of the cross, which for them represented the sacred ceiba tree, supporting the thirteen heavens, and with roots penetrating the nine levels of the underworld.

Human sacrifice and idolatry were widespread among the Postclassic

Maya encountered by the conquistadors in the Yucatán; but sacrifice on a major scale was almost certainly an import from the Toltecs.

There is some confusion over the role of Kukulcan or Quetzalcoatl, a mythical invader from Mexico, said to have arrived in the Maya area in Postclassic times, and who is variously credited with forbidding human sacrifice and idolatry, and with introducing these practices. In fact, human sacrifice was apparently practised in Classic times, as depicted on numerous stelae at Tikal and elsewhere, though on a smaller scale than subsequently. In addition, there are instances of burials of decapitated or ritually mutilated victims going back to Preclassic times, but it is unclear whether the victims were sacrificed, or executed as criminals or prisoners of war.

The growing complexity of Maya beliefs and ritual practices came to need a professional priesthood, organized in a complex hierarchy. In the early days, religious observances were performed by individual householders or part-time specialists. But the development of Maya ritual, calendrics, astronomy, and esoteric knowledge required and justified the presence of an élite priestly class, in whose interests it was to reinforce the divide between themselves and the common people.

In the same way as no distinction was made between the seen and unseen worlds, so was there no distinction made between temporal and priestly power. The chief priest was invariably also the ruler: the power he held over the unseen world, exercised through divination and ritual, was fundamental to his kingly responsibilities. The extraordinary cultural development of the Classic Maya both required and resulted in this centralization of power.

Since that power was broken – first with the fall of the Classic Maya, then seven centuries later with the Spanish Conquest, the Maya knowledge and culture has ebbed away like water from a broken pot. Maya traditions do live on in remote villages, and the outlook of the indigenous Maya populations of southern Mexico and Guatemala remains fundamentally different from that of the dominant Spanish speakers. But the glory of the Classic Maya remains, for them as much as for us, in the remote and forgotten past.

3   The Ruins of Tikal

The Temple of the Great Jaguar

Looking out from Tikal's Temple I, the Temple of the Great Jaguar, the jungle below is a sea of green to the distant horizon. Small clouds and their dark trailing shadows move slowly over the sunlit expanse. The four limestone hulls of the other great temple pyramids tower over the trees, smaller structures mostly concealed by the waves of foliage. The cries of elusive toucans and spider monkeys echo up as they dart around the upper branches. The air is fresh at this level with cool breezes, and the maddening mosquitoes do not fly so high.

Moving clockwise around the horizon, facing Temple I over the Great Plaza, the heart of Tikal, stands the slightly lower Temple II. Half a mile further west over the trees is Tikal's greatest temple, Temple IV, facing back towards the centre. Temple III lies between the Plaza and Temple IV, just to the south. On the north side of the Plaza stands the North Acropolis, a vast raised platform, bearing the remains of some twelve major temples, and other smaller structures. Behind Temple I, half a mile to the east, is the disused airstrip by the hotel and museum zone. To the south, and stretching eastwards, is the Central Acropolis, a mass of interlinked palaces and courtyards, still partly covered by trees and jungle growth.

The last of the five great temples, Temple V, is due south of Temple I, facing towards the Great Plaza, over the palaces of the Central Acropolis and a large reservoir, now just a dip in the trees. Next to Temple V is the enormous bulk of the unexcavated South Acropolis, covered in trees, like a natural hill dominating the whole site.

Additional complexes of pyramids, palaces and other structures lie further out. They were once linked to the centre by wide processional causeways, each named for one of the early explorers. These complexes are more prosaically known by letters of the alphabet, with individual buildings numbered according to their position on a grid used by archaeologists. The three main causeways form a triangle of about half a mile on each side. The Maler Causeway leads due north from behind Temple I, to the North Zone on a hill about half a mile away. From here, the Maudslay Causeway, up to 200 feet wide in places, runs south west to Temple IV. The triangle is completed by the east-west Tozzer Causeway back to the Great Plaza. A fourth causeway is the Mendez, which leads south-east from behind Temple I to the Temple of the

Polychrome plate in the Tikal Museum, of unknown provenance. It was recovered by the Guatemalan armed forces in a swoop on smugglers trying to leave the country with a rich haul of looted Maya artefacts destined for 'collectors' in the United States and elsewhere. Tikal itself is relatively safe from grave-robbers, but the countless lesser sites in the Petén cannot all be protected.

Inscriptions, about 1 mile out into the jungle. The route of the causeways cannot be seen from the temple, although there are plans to clear them of growth.

Further away on the horizon to the north-west is a range of low limestone hills. The white rock is exposed in places and clearly visible from a great distance. All around are depressions formed by the bajos, lakes that once surrounded Tikal but are now long dry. In the rainy season they flood easily, forming areas of swamps.

The basic orientation of Tikal, located by the five temples and the triangle of causeways, should be simple. In practice, it is easy to get lost along the jungle paths, as it is impossible to see more than a few yards through the thick growth. A compass and a good map (or a guide) are vital, even for a thorough one-day visit. The sequence of this chapter broadly follows the triangle of the causeways, moving clockwise, and starting at the Great Plaza in front of Temple I. The map opposite shows the central area around the Great Plaza, while the larger-scale map on page 77 shows the whole site.

The Great Plaza is now reached by a twisting jungle track, much used by flocks of wild turkeys. The track runs from the hotel area, and past the side of Temple I. In its days of glory, the Plaza was reached by a grand stairway along the north side, some 75 yards wide, leading up to the terrace in front of the temples of the massive North Acropolis. Approached from the jungle, the Plaza, with its smooth grass floor, gives an immediate impression of space. Underfoot lie four layers of stucco flooring, in places up to 2 feet thick. The earliest layer dates from around 150 BC, the latest from AD 750; each time from major rebuilding was carried out around the Plaza, a new floor was laid.

At 145 feet, Temple I and its towering roof-comb dominate the Plaza from the east. It is also known as the Temple of the Great Jaguar, for the carving of a jaguar on one of the door lintels. The temple is a typical but magnificent Late Classic building, dating from around AD 720, and was constructed over the tomb of Tikal's greatest ruler, Ah Cacau. Nine stepped and corniced terraces, representing the nine lords of the underworld, support a building platform, which carries a temple building of three narrow parallel chambers, spanned by corbel vaults.

A steep and narrow stairway runs up the front of the temple to the chambers. This was closed to the public at the time of writing, pending a major restoration project planned for the early 1990s. It was actually

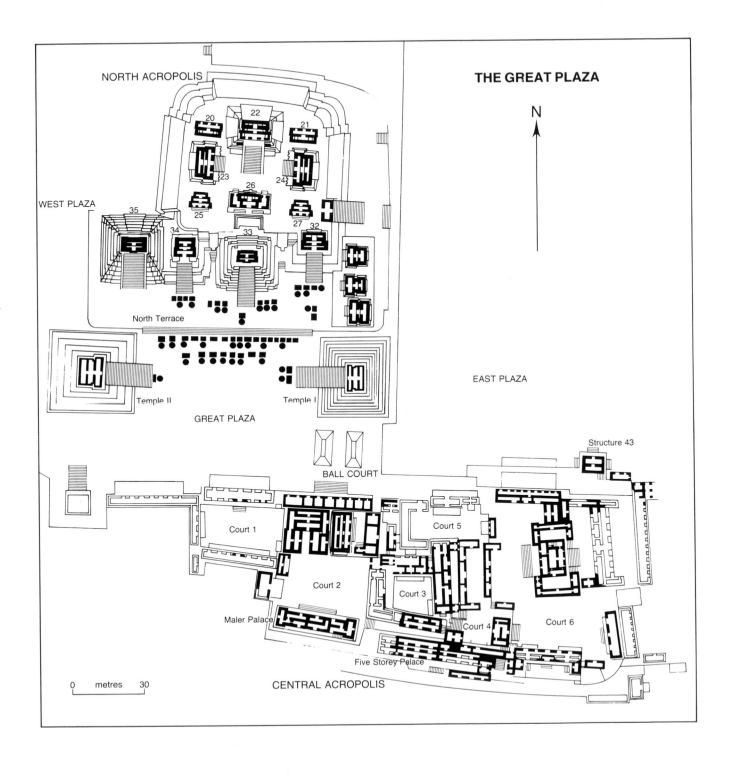

THE GREAT PLAZA

N

NORTH ACROPOLIS

WEST PLAZA

North Terrace

EAST PLAZA

Temple II

Temple I

GREAT PLAZA

BALL COURT

Structure 43

Court 1

Court 5

Court 2

Court 3

Court 6

Maler Palace

Court 4

0   metres   30

Five Storey Palace

CENTRAL ACROPOLIS

a construction stair, built over with a wide ceremonial stair at the final stage, after completion of other building work; remains of the main stair can be seen at the foot of the temple.

The doorways between the chambers are spanned by multi-beam lintels of sapodilla, a tough hardwood. As with all of Tikal's temples, the lintels to the outer door are plain, but with intricate carvings on those to the inner doors. Two of the four beams to the middle door are still in place, while the others were removed in the nineteenth century to London and Switzerland and replaced with replicas. The rear walls support the bulk of the roof-comb, which was built in two stages with a hollow chamber sealed inside to reduce its weight. On the front of the comb is the eroded carving of a seated figure and serpent, once painted in red, green and cream, but hard to discern now except with the long shadows of the setting sun.

Tunnelling under Temple I by archaeologists of the Tikal Project uncovered the tomb of Ah Cacau, known as Burial 116. This was the richest burial found at Tikal, and the treasures are now displayed in the National Museum in Guatemala City, with a replica of the burial in the Tikal Museum. On Ah Cacau's body alone were found some 180 pieces of jade ornament. Other artefacts included bone carved with glyphs and scenes, delicately painted pottery showing Ah Cacau's journey to the underworld in a canoe rowed by animals, pearls, seashells, and the stingray spines that were used for ritual blood-letting. Nor was Ah Cacau the only occupant of Temple I. An important individual, perhaps one of his descendants, seems to have been buried at a later date in a tomb beneath the rear chamber. Unfortunately, this was looted by the Postclassic Maya, who then re-used the tomb for one of their chiefs, leaving various red hand prints of unknown significance on the walls of the temple.

A few yards to the south of Temple I is a small ball-court, one of three at Tikal, and the smallest found in Mesoamerica. The game was played by two opposing teams, with a hard rubber ball, the aim being to knock it through a stone hoop using elbows and hips. The size of the court suggests that it may have been used by children, perhaps temple acolytes or page boys.

Facing Temple I across the Plaza is Temple II, similar but shorter, with only three stepped terraces supporting the building platform. This is known as the Temple of the Masks, for the two eroded masks that

Rear view of Temple III's roof-comb, which reaches some 180 feet above the jungle floor. The temple was completed in AD 810, probably as the funerary monument to Tikal's last known ruler, Chitam. Like all the major temples, it was completely stuccoed, and painted red, cream and green. No doubt the central mask panel seen here was highlighted so as to be visible for many miles, staring out across the jungle.

flank the upper central stair. At the same level, a large stone platform projects over the stairs; this commands a view of the whole Plaza, and was no doubt used by priests to address a throng below. The plain 12-foot stela at the foot of the stair is the largest found at Tikal, and was reconstructed from shattered pieces.

The eroded lintel in the middle chamber shows a woman, supposed to be the wife of Ah Cacau, and the temple may have been dedicated to her. Part of the lintel is now in the Museum of Natural History in New York. On the stucco of the chambers, Postclassic peoples incised scenes of warfare, but these have been largely covered with more modern graffiti. No tomb was found at Temple II, but an important burial (no. 196) was beneath the flat-topped and overgrown pyramid just to the south of Temple II. Similar to Ah Cacau's burial, this was probably that of his son, Yax Kin. The finest single piece found here was a jade jaguar weighing some 4 lb, now in the Tikal Museum. This temple probably had a wood and thatch temple enclosure, and the Postclassic graffiti in Temple II showed exactly such a construction.

Out into the Plaza, and to the south-east of Temple II a three-chamber chultún (an artificial cave hollowed from the bed rock) was found. For conservation reasons, its entrance has been closed off. At least 300 such chambers have been identified at Tikal, and their purpose is the subject of much speculation. Some were used for burials, but this may not have been their original purpose. The storage of water or food has also been suggested.

On the north of the Plaza and on the North Terrace, there are some 70 carved and plain stelae and altars in rows, some protected by thatched roofs. Most of the finer carved monuments have now been taken to the Tikal Museum, but there are plans to place replicas in the original locations. Most of the stelae date from the Early Classic period, but few are in their original locations, having been re-erected by Postclassic peoples occupying the site. The few Late Classic stelae are larger, more symmetrical, and have rounded rather than square tops. Several stelae bear traces of red paint, and it is likely that all were painted this colour. In various cases, stelae have been defaced; this seems to have been a common practice after the death or disgrace of a ruler or dynasty. Some disfacement may date from Postclassic times.

Of particular interest is Stela 5 (AD 744), on the North Terrace. The front bears a portrait of Yax Kin, wearing an ornate feather head-dress,

Above left Stucco mask of the Maya rain god, uncovered during excavation of the North Acropolis. It originally flanked a stair, and was preserved by one of the frequent rebuildings of the acropolis, walled in behind new terraces. It was deliberately damaged before the rebuilding, for unknown reasons.

Below left The main stairway to Temple 32 in the North Acropolis. To the right are two small Early Classic temples, which face in over the North Terrace of the Great Plaza. They have not been excavated, and may well contain further tombs with offerings, which await future generations of archaeologists.

Above right View from the building in the centre of Court 6 in the Central Acropolis, looking west over the smaller Court 4, and to the upper part of the Five Storey Palace.

Below right The upper galleries of the Five Storey Palace in the Central Acropolis. This part of the building was constructed in the seventh century, and the lower stories, stepping out down the side of the ravine beside the acropolis, were added later.

Far left The powerful trunk of a ceiba tree, sacred to the Maya, and now a national symbol for Guatemala. Around Tikal there are many ceibas, some growing on the sides of pyramids, their roots prying apart huge masonry blocks, their upper branches higher than all but the roof-combs of the great temples.

Left Creeper and parasitic vines overwhelm a ceiba tree in the rainforest.

and standing on a bound prisoner. On the side of the stela are intricate glyphs, while the top of its nearby altar, although eroded, shows a second prisoner awaiting sacrifice. Stela 7 (AD 495), nearby on the east end of the North Terrace, shows the ruler Jaguar Paw I, with a clear example of the Tikal emblem glyph on the left side; the stela has been reassembled from fragments. Down on the Plaza, Stela 10 (AD 527) is the seventh from the left in the second row. It shows a ruler thought to be Curl Head, again standing on a bound prisoner. Stela 11 is in the same row, and is the latest dated monument at Tikal, from AD 869; the ruler shown is unknown. Altar 4, on the right of the North Terrace, shows carvings of a monkey, a symbol of promiscuity.

This area around the Great Plaza was the focus of Tikal's religious life, and undoubtedly the scene of complex rituals and ceremonies, with crowds, sounds and costumes that would put to shame any Hollywood epic. The coronation and funerals of rulers, observance of calendrical changes, worship of the gods, the sacrifice of prisoners after victory in war, and other rites that we can only guess at: all would have been enacted here. It is hard for the imagination to bring it all to life, with the temples painted in red, green and other colours. But the serenity of the ruins today should not hide how alien and remote it was from the experience of our own civilization.

The Three Acropoli

The North Acropolis is an enormous raised platform on the north side of the Great Plaza, bearing twelve major temples. It went through at least three major rebuildings during the Classic period, the final platform level being some 45 feet above the level of the Plaza, and extending over almost 2½ acres. The earliest constructions, revealed by deep trenching through the platform, date back to 100 BC. We do not know the dedicatory deities of the temples, but at least 80 funeral chambers of nobles and priests have been uncovered in the acropolis, with many more small caches of ritual offerings. The veneration of ancestors must thus have been a major purpose of the temples.

A row of four temples faces the Great Plaza over the North Terrace. They are known only by their numbers, 35–32, running from left to right. Temple 35, on the left, is largely unrestored, and was added to the main body of the acropolis in the Late Classic era. The Early Classic

Temple 34 is partly restored, and its architectural style shows several of the features which would develop into the full Classic of Temples I and II, such as the use of apron mouldings on the terracing. Beneath Temple IV the tomb of Tikal's Early Classic ruler Curl Nose was found, together with nine retainers who were clearly despatched to the underworld in company with their lord. The Red Stela (no. 26), now in the new Tikal Museum, and thought to record the accession of Jaguar Paw Skull II around AD 530, was also uncovered here, partly smashed and built into the rear wall of the temple chamber.

At the centre is the larger Temple 33, its three superimposed structures fully excavated and explored. Sadly, the latest construction, about the same size as Temple II, was in poor condition, and was dismantled by archaeologists after much controversy. Only the bottom steps remain, and the visible structure dates from the Early Classic. Various large decorative stucco masks were preserved by the rebuilding, and are now protected by thatch covers. The largest is 10 feet high, with access through an old archaeological excavation trench. Temple 33 contained the burial of Tikal's great early Classic ruler, Stormy Sky; also found here was Stela 31 (now in the old Tikal Museum), damaged and buried in the Late Classic period, but still revealing key historical and dynastic information.

Temple 32, on the right of the acropolis, has been restored, and dates from the Late Classic period. Burial 32 found here has not been identified to a ruler, but contained the remarkable blue stucco figurines of the Rain God now in the old Tikal Museum. To the right of Temple 32 is a small row of three small unrestored temples. Behind in the main body of the acropolis are eight Early Classic temples arranged in a square, the three on the east restored, contrasting with their unrestored twins on the west. The best view of the whole complex is from the upper part of the rear central temple as it catches the last rays of the evening sun.

Down a short stairway passing between Temple II and the west of the North Acropolis is the largely unexcavated West Plaza, with the mounds of Late Classic temples and palaces on its north and west. One small temple on the west is of particular archaeological interest, as the only unfinished structure found at Tikal, possible evidence of the sudden collapse.

The 4 acres of Tikal's second great acropolis, the Central Acro-

Overleaf Temples I and II seen over the canopy of trees from the platform of Temple IV.

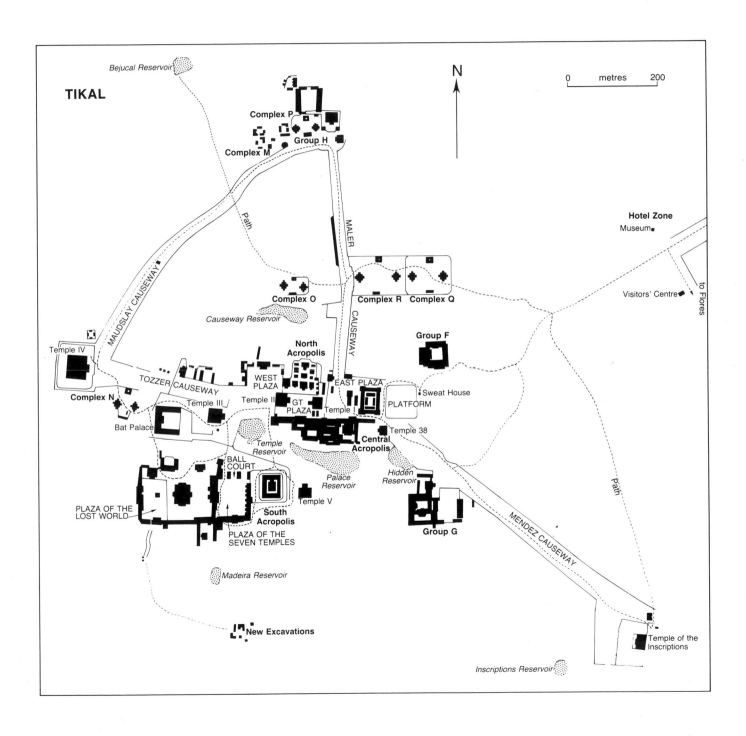

TIKAL

N

0   metres   200

Bejucal Reservoir

Complex P

Complex M

Group H

Path

MALER

Hotel Zone
Museum

CAUSEWAY

Complex O

Complex R   Complex Q

Visitors' Centre

to Flores

Causeway Reservoir

MAUDSLAY CAUSEWAY

North
Acropolis

Group F

Temple IV

WEST
PLAZA

EAST PLAZA

Sweat House

TOZZER CAUSEWAY

Complex N

Temple III

Temple II

GT
PLAZA

Temple I

PLATFORM

Temple 38

Path

Bat Palace

Temple
Reservoir

Central
Acropolis

BALL
COURT

Palace
Reservoir

Hidden
Reservoir

PLAZA OF THE
LOST WORLD

Temple V

MENDEZ CAUSEWAY

South
Acropolis

Group G

PLAZA OF THE
SEVEN TEMPLES

Madeira Reservoir

New Excavations

Temple of the
Inscriptions

Inscriptions Reservoir

polis, run along the south sides of the Great and East Plazas. Its overall length is some 700 feet, with forty-two major buildings around six main courtyards on different levels, the courts numbered sequentially from west to east. Unlike the North Acropolis, the Central consists almost entirely of single and multi-story vaulted 'palace' buildings, rather than temples, and apparently contains no major burials. As ever, the acropolis was built in many accretive stages, with earlier buildings buried under the latest constructions; the bedrock is up to 50 feet below the level of the courts. The reasonable speculation is that the acropolis was the residential quarter for priests and nobles, although it is not clear how sanitation was arranged. Some parts of the acropolis formed a labyrinth of stairs, passages and secret courts, so that each area could have housed a different dynastic group or part of the priestly hierarchy, in absolute privacy.

Court 1 to the west is unrestored, apart from the side facing the West Plaza and the building dividing it from Court 2. A path runs up to Court 2, which can also be reached directly from the Great Plaza, up a narrow stair to the right of a long narrow palace on an intermediate level. Court 2 has been substantially restored, most notably the two-storey Maler's Palace on the south side, named for the famous early archaeologist, who lived here during his excavations.

The upper part of the building bears the remains of a decorative frieze, which encircled many buildings of the acropolis. Just inside the doorways are holes in the stonework, which may have held rails for curtains; there is no evidence that doors were used. The interior stuccoed walls have been much defaced by graffiti, both by Postclassic Maya, and by modern tourists. Maler himself incised his name on the left side of the middle door. An external stair to the rear leads to the roof, where the great comb of Temple v can be seen, looking out over the deep depression in the jungle that was the Palace Reservoir. This was the largest of central Tikal's twelve such reservoirs, all lined with clay and fed by rainwater channels.

Three low palaces form the north side of Court 2; the one to the west has a U-shaped plan, and the remains of small roof-combs, unusual for a palace building. Court 3 is lower, and unrestored except for the Five Storey Palace on its southern side. The top two storeys are now home to a family of 'zopilote' vultures, who greatly resent the intrusion of visitors. The bottom storeys are terraced down the steep side of the

reservoir, with a series of external stairs leading down to a platform overlooking the reservoir.

Courts 4 and 5, on the south and north sides of the acropolis respectively, are smaller, and largely unrestored. On the east both give on to the irregularly shaped Court 6, the largest of the acropolis, and known also as the Great East Court. On the west of the court is a series of three palaces with long, thin galleries, while to the east is a large and complex palace on a platform, with a well-preserved section of decorative frieze. The central part of the palace is Early Classic, while the wings date from a later period; the smaller stones of the central part are a good clue to the dating. The northern wing has a unique feature at Tikal, an interior winding staircase linking the two storeys; it is not known why Maya architects were so reluctant to use this undoubtedly convenient device.

North of Court 6 is the East Plaza, a large and mostly unexcavated area described later in the chapter. From the western end of the Central Acropolis, a signposted path leads south to Temple V, another of the great pyramids, with a single narrow temple chamber crowning its steep 188-foot bulk. Only the chamber and comb have been consolidated, with further work under way at the time of writing. The pyramid itself is covered by trees, with tangled roots that provide convenient hand-holds. The front of the comb was stuccoed with mask motifs, but only traces of this remain. Around Temple V is the best place to see spider monkeys, which come out to feed in the late afternoon with much chattering and shrieking.

Immediately to the west of Temple V is the huge tree-covered mass of the South Acropolis, which dominates the whole centre and which has barely been explored, let alone restored. The base covers 5 acres, making it the largest of the three acropoli, and it seems to have been far simpler in concept than the other two, with a series of huge superimposed square platforms, stepping up asymmetrically to a courtyard of palaces, which encircled a central temple at the summit. A climb up the South Acropolis is best left to archaeologists, as little can be seen.

Jungle paths skirt both the north and south of the acropolis, leading west to the Plaza of the Seven Temples, named for the row of seven small Late Classic temples on its east side. Although they are unrestored, an interesting skull motif can be discerned on the upper

The moon rises over Temples I, II, and III, seen from Temple IV.

Above The Pyramid of the Lost World, seen from Temple IV as sunset approaches.

Above right The main palace complex at Palenque, centred around the unique four-storey tower with interior stairs – it was probably used for astronomical observation. The buildings are mostly Late Classic, but the style is very different to that of Tikal. Relatively large interior spaces are covered by mansarded roofs that were once stuccoed and covered with beautifully carved bas-reliefs. There is none of Tikal's overwhelming monumentality, but a strong impression of architectural harmony prevails.

Below right The temple enclosure of Twin Pyramid Complex Q at Tikal, seen through the typical single-arched gateway. The complex was built under Chitam, Tikal's last known ruler, in AD 771. Stela 22 in the centre shows the ruler in the flamboyant head-dress favoured by the Maya nobility.

façade of the central temple. Two reasonably intact larger temples stand on the west side, and on the north is an unusual triple court for playing the sacred ball-game.

Further to the west is the recently restored Plaza of the Lost World. In the centre of the plaza stands a 100-foot square plan pyramid, with intricate stairs and terraces flanked by stucco masks. Only the western half has been restored, while the top has no temple chamber, and may have carried a temple of wood and thatch. A smaller, similar pyramid stands on the north-west of the plaza, with a low building platform in the same style to its south.

From the south-west of the plaza, a path leads over a bridge to an area of recent excavation about 500 yards south-east into the jungle. Work has now halted, but an interesting structure has been uncovered, with an especially fine stucco serpent head painted in a well-preserved green. Returning to the Lost World, a path leads north to the 180-foot pyramid of Temple III, also known as the Temple of the Jaguar Priest. Like Temple V, Temple III has only been consolidated at the top, but can be climbed. At the south-east of the pyramid base stand Stela 24 and Altar 6, dated to AD 810. The carvings on the altar show evidence of human sacrifice, with a human head shown on a tripod bowl. The temple has only two chambers, and its carved door lintel is the largest remaining in Tikal. It is possible to make out the figure of a very fat man dressed in jaguar skins, and wearing a feather head-dress.

Along the Four Causeways

Away from the centre of the site visitors are few, and the jungle wildlife more plentiful; in most of the ruins described below, the only company will be lizards basking in the sun on the old stones.

From the north side of Temple III, a path leads west. This follows the course of the Tozzer Causeway, once a ceremonial avenue, with a smooth stucco floor up to 300 feet in width. Almost immediately to the south is the Bat Palace, also known as the Palace of the Windows for the narrow openings on its west front. From the upper storey, the mask panel on the rear of Temple III's roof-comb can be clearly seen. Just to the west, and still on the south of the causeway, stand the twin pyramid complexes and related buildings named Complex N.

Nine similar groups are known at Tikal, built during the Late Classic

The precarious wooden ladders leading up the overgrown terraces of Temple IV, the tallest standing pyramid of all Mesoamerica. Cold drink vendors cluster round the base, waiting for thirsty climbers to descend.

era to mark the passing of 20-year periods. The pattern is common: two identical pyramids about 100 yards apart on an east-west axis, with a small enclosure to the north containing a stela and altar, and a small shrine to the south. Complex N dates from AD 711, and its Stela 16 shows Ah Cacau, Tikal's greatest ruler, with Altar 5 showing two priests by an altar bearing a skull and a bone. Both are in the museum, with replicas in situ.

The causeway continues west to the base of Temple IV, the latest and tallest of Tikal's pyramid temples at 208 feet, completed around AD 741 under the ruler Yax Kin. The masonry and fill used in its construction weigh around one million tonnes. They were taken from numerous quarries in the surrounding jungle. The seven terraces remain covered by trees, but the three-room temple and comb, reached by a series of wooden ladders, have been restored. The carved lintels were removed to Switzerland in the nineteenth century. A final metal ladder allows the brave to reach the base of the comb; the mask panel at the rear can be seen by edging around the parapet. Temple IV is the favoured spot for watching the sun drop spectacularly below the jungle horizon, although this involves a return to the hotel area in fading light.

From Temple IV, a path leads up along the Maudsley Causeway to the recently excavated North Zone, about 800 yards to the north-east. In places, remains of the causeway and its parapets can be seen through the jungle. The causeway arrives directly to a plaza, with a partly restored temple facing east. North of the plaza is a typical twin pyramid group, dated to AD 751, with an altar depicting a bound prisoner awaiting sacrifice. Further north again, a larger temple on a raised platform faces south down the Maler Causeway, back towards the central area.

The Maler Causeway is the best preserved of the causeways, with the parapets clearly visible in several places. Just as it leaves the North Zone, descending steeply, a carved rock face on the west side shows two bound prisoners. After about 400 yards, an intersecting path leads west to Complex O, and east to Complexes R and Q, three twin pyramid groups. Only Complex Q has been substantially restored, and has the superb Stela 22, showing the accession of Chitam, Tikal's last known ruler, in AD 771. From Complex Q, a path leads back to the hotels. This area is inhabited by families of large jungle rodents like coypus, undisturbed in their feeding by all but the noisiest visitors.

The front of Stela 10 in the Great Plaza, tentatively dated to AD 527, and thought to show the ruler Curl Head. Much detail has been lost through erosion, but parts of his costume can be seen, as can a bound prisoner, belly down behind his feet, probably awaiting sacrifice.

Panel of glyphs on Stela 21, by the Temple of the Inscriptions. The stela was carved during the rule of Yax Kin, the glyphs giving a date of AD 736. It was discovered in 1951 by Guatemalan soldiers hunting for game; it had tipped forward, shattering the head over an altar at its base. The lower parts, including this panel, were preserved in the stela's fallen position.

The right side of Stela 31, in the Visitors' Centre. The bottom right-hand glyph is a version of Tikal's emblem glyph. The figure is of a warrior from Teotihuacán, carrying a spear thrower. Stormy Sky, in whose reign the stela was carved, may have depended on Teotihuacán mercenaries to expand Tikal's power.

Cast resin copy of the carved wooden lintel from Temple IV in the Guatemala City Museum of Archaeology. The original is in Basel, Switzerland, but only an expert could tell the difference. Since the museum's exhibits are almost completely unlabelled, most who see the piece are none the wiser. The lintel has been dated to AD 741, and almost certainly shows the ruler Yax Kin in full regalia.

The path continues south, arriving in the East Plaza behind Temple I. The most notable structure in the small cleared part of the plaza is Structure 43, jutting out from the north side of the Central Acropolis; the architectural style is non-Maya, with the decorated panels reminiscent of Teotihuacán in the Valley of Mexico. But most of the plaza's 5 acres and many buildings remain under jungle, including a large ball-court, a square group of plain buildings known speculatively as the Market Place, and a mysterious 400-foot square platform apparently carrying no buildings. This may have been a parade ground, or may have been awaiting a grandiose construction project that for some reason never took place. Alternatively, it may have been covered in wood and thatch buildings. A path leads north-east around the side of this platform to the overgrown buildings of Group F. Puzzlingly, a small steam-bath house stands by the east side of the platform; it may have been used for ceremonial purification by priests. Similar constructions are used by the modern highland Maya for the same purpose.

The fourth of the causeways, the Mendez, leads south-east from the East Plaza, passing almost at once on the right the large unrestored Late Classic Temple 38. A number of human skulls were discovered here in the shrine halfway up the stairway, further evidence of human sacrifice at Tikal. A short distance further down the causeway, again to the right, stands the recently restored Group G, consisting of large palaces build around five courts. Two of the courts have been reconstructed, and the large mask of a monster which opens to the tunnel leading to the eastern of the two is particularly interesting. The largest palace is known as the 'Palace of the Channels', for the vertical channel motifs of unknown purposes on its walls.

Half a mile down the causeway is the Temple of the Inscriptions, the last of the great temples, only discovered in 1951. The rear of its 40-foot roof-comb is covered with heavily eroded glyphic inscriptions, believed to relate the history of Tikal. At the base of the pyramid is Stela 21, dated AD 766. This has finely carved date glyphs, but has been shattered and defaced so that only the foot of the depicted ruler remains. Other plain stelae and altars lie all around, entangled in the massive roots of ceiba trees. A path leads directly back to the hotel and museum zone, a ½ mile away.

There are two museums near the hotels. The new Visitors' Centre is

One of the wild turkeys that roam in flocks around the Tikal National Park, safe from hunters. The iridescent feathers were prized by the Maya for head-dresses and costumes; the flesh was no doubt a delicacy for ceremonial feasts.

Above right Stone bed in a building of the Central Acropolis, presumably used for sleeping, although not reaching modern standards of double-sprung comfort.

Below right Terraces and temple at Yaxchilán, a major Classic centre on the river Usumacinta, which seems to have been within Tikal's sphere of influence during parts of the Classic period.

an airy modern building containing some twenty-five of the finest stelae and altars from all over the site. One stela on display is of unknown provenance, and was recovered by the Guatemalan customs as it was being smuggled out of the county; only the face was found, as the rear had been sawn off to save weight in an astonishing display of vandalistic greed. The locally available book, *The Rulers of Tikal*, by Genevieve Michel, is recommended reading while passing the heat of the day examining the exhibits in detail. The museum's large, plaster scale-model of central Tikal makes possible a leap of the imagination, from today's jungle-covered ruins back to the days of Tikal's glory. A similar model is also on display in the Anthropology Museum in Guatemala City.

The second and older museum contains artefacts from Tikal's burials. The museum was raided in 1981, supposedly by guerrillas who removed the best jade pieces, probably now in the hands of private 'collectors' in the United States. Many fine pieces remain, of jade, mosaic, painted ceramic, and carved bone, although the display methods are antiquated. Various other pieces from Tikal are on display in the museum in Guatemala City, poorly lit and without proper labels or explanation.

Terraces and platforms at Uaxactún, some 15 miles to the north of Tikal. Although extensive, the city has hardly been excavated, and was dominated by Tikal during most of its existence.

4   Fall, Revival and Conquest

The Fall of Tikal

By AD 1000, the delicate balance of society and nature that sustained Tikal had been shattered. Tikal and the other lowland Classic cities had been deserted. Further north in the Yucatán the Maya collapse was less dramatic, but there too the signs of cultural decline are present. At the same time, the Zapotecs in the Valley of Oaxaca were succumbing to Mixtec invaders. The power of Teotihuacán had long faded, and the Valley of Mexico was now dominated by the militaristic Toltecs from their capital at Tula. The Classic civilizations had drawn to an end, giving way to the more turbulent Postclassic era.

The Classic Maya collapse has preoccupied Mayanists since the earliest days. The first theories concentrated on establishing a single devastating cause, a war, a drought, an epidemic, a rebellion, or a sudden failure of agriculture. But these explanations do not fit with the archaeological facts. Rather, there was a process of decline and fall, spreading from one centre to the next, spanning a period of about a century. The fall of Tikal is a good starting point. It was the single major event in the Maya collapse, and happened rapidly, with a drastic fall in population over a single generation. There is, however, no evidence of a cataclysmic end.

This lack of conclusive evidence has given rise to diverse theories. Convincing arguments have been made that there was an ecological collapse through over-farming, with deforestation leading to soil erosion and water shortages. The fertile lands around Tikal are known to be prone to erosion; in a time of crisis, destructive over-exploitation of land and forest would have been likely. One theory is that the former lakes became silted up with sediment from over-intensive agriculture. Supporting evidence for this comes from deep accumulations of silt found in the bajos, and the results would have been devastating.

Another, although not exclusive, possibility is that of a peasants' revolt. Much of the food they grew would have been taken for the priestly élite and those servicing their needs. When not working in the fields, the same peasants provided the labour for ever more ambitious building works for the glory of their rulers. The evidence of skeletal remains shows that labouring people were several inches smaller than the élite, and had a shorter life expectancy. Towards the end, it seems that the common people endured a monotonous and inadequate diet and water shortages. There is a limit to human endurance, and

The east façade of the Magician's Pyramid at Uxmal, which faces the Nunnery Quadrangle. Masks of the rain god flank the stair, stepping back along the slope of the pyramid. The House of the Magician was the last addition, at the top. It was built on the roof of an earlier temple, the doorway of which is formed by the mouth of a large 'Chenes'-style stone mosaic mask, again of the rain god. Given the arid climate, and the shortage of surface water, the cult of the rain god was enormously important to the people of Uxmal. Down on the bottom left side are the remains of the earliest construction, unearthed by archaeologists.

Overleaf A serpent head and a standing figure flanking the main stairway to the Temple of the Warriors at Chichén Itzá. The figure is a standard-bearer, designed to hold a pole for a flag or blazon. This feature is not found at Maya sites of any period, but is common at centres built by the Toltecs and the much later Aztecs.

discontent among the peasantry may well have been a factor in undermining Classic Maya civilization.

As well as these internal problems, there were also threats from outside, specifically from the Chontal or Putún Maya, a people from the old Olmec homeland on the Gulf coast. They had come to control the vital maritime trade route around the Yucatán coast to the Caribbean, bypassing the more arduous inland routes. They had also become Mexicanized through their trading contacts with the Toltecs in the Valley of Mexico.

By the end of the Classic period the Chontal had begun to penetrate the Maya heartland, moving up the rivers and taking over vulnerable centres. Among the first to fall were the sites of Altar de Sacrificios and Seibal along the Usumacinta river. These appear to have come under foreign influence around AD 771. Mexicanized ceramics from Tabasco first enter the archaeological record at Altar, and are found several decades later at Seibal, just 60 miles from Tikal. The foreign influence at Seibal appears to have triggered a cultural flowering from AD 830 to 890, with the many fine monuments from this period showing a distinct Mexican influence. One stela seems to show the surrender of Seibal's Maya ruler to a long-haired warrior, one of the Chontal invaders.

Not everywhere fared so well: at Piedras Negras, another Usumacinta site, a regular sequence of monuments commemorating each 5-year period of the Long Count calendar came to an end in AD 810. Yaxchilán, the dominant Usumacinta centre during the Classic period, left its last dated monument in AD 807. The growth of the favoured sites, such as Seibal, was to the detriment of the former established centres, such as Tikal.

By the time that Chitam, Tikal's last known ruler, came to power in AD 768, Tikal had been a major ceremonial centre for nearly 1,000 years. A period of major construction was at its peak, and the population had grown considerably to build and then service the central palaces and temples, with their ever-growing number of priests, nobles, administrators and merchants. But this expansion had pushed the agricultural support system to the limits of sustainability. Worse, the constant need for wood to fire the limestone needed for stucco, and to stoke the kilns for an increasingly industrialized ceramics production, had denuded large areas of forest, exposing the soil to erosion.

For a time, things remained stable. Although dependent on some vital

imports, such as salt from the Yucatán, Tikal was just able to balance its resource budget and keep open the vital trade routes. Perhaps the mass-production methods applied to ceramics were also applied to other products, such as textiles or carved wood, for export to pay for food imports. Tikal may even have maintained military outposts to ensure access to vital strategic resources. But the resource balance was increasingly delicate; with the inroads of the aggressive mercantile power of the Chontal, that balance was eventually destroyed.

With the undermining of Tikal's economy through the collapse of trade, other factors such as ecological destruction and peasant unrest would have become critical and mutually reinforcing. Many of Tikal's people must have died of thirst and malnutrition or disease, with others melting away into the jungle. Some smaller centres nearby grew at Tikal's expense, and it was in one of these, Jimbal, that the latest monument in the Tikal area has been found, with a date of AD 889. Soon, large areas of Tikal were uninhabited, buildings quickly becoming smothered in tropical growth. Within a few decades, only small groups of survivors remained in the centre, attempting unsuccessfully to maintain the old traditions. It was not long before the site was completely abandoned. After 1,000 years, the jungle reclaimed Tikal.

Maya Revival

After the collapse of the great lowland centres, the Yucatán peninsula became the focus of a revived but Mexican-influenced Postclassic Maya civilization. Established centres such as Dzibilchaltún, near Mérida, continued to flourish and expand, and new centres, such as Chichen Itzá, were founded. To a lesser extent, the Guatemalan highlands also experienced something of a revival, accompanied by an incursion of Mexican influence which is reflected in the local art and architecture. Mexican influence also reached the Yucatán, but probably not, as has long been thought, as the result of a full-scale Toltec invasion. More likely is that the Mexicanized Chontal Maya who had destabilized the Classic Maya civilization extended their influence into the remainder of the Maya area.

Little is known of the Chontals' origin, but they may have been the descendants of the Olmec: certainly they inhabited the same territory. By the close of the Classic period, the Chontal had become thoroughly

Right Stela 2 at Seibal, a Late Classic site on the Río de la Pasión in the Petén. After the fall of Tikal, Seibal expanded its influence, but seems to have been conquered by invaders from the northern Maya area, who brought with them Mexican influences. The orange colour of the stone comes from a persistent strain of algae that flourishes in the damp jungle climate. The style of the stela is distinctly Mexican, showing a ruler wearing a monkey mask and an ornate head-dress.

Above Bas-relief from the sloping sides of the main ball-court at Chichén Itzá. The captain of the victorious team holds the severed head of the opposing captain in one hand, and a racket or bat in the other. It is claimed that on the special occasions involved, the victims went willingly, even eagerly, to be sacrificed, regarding it as an honour. Even so, one can imagine that they played for more than just the satisfaction of a good game on such days. Eight other ball-courts are known to have existed at Chichén, and the game must have been a dominant factor in the life of the city.

Above left The Temple of the Jaguar, which faces on to the Chichén Itzá ball-court, almost like a pavilion for spectators. In the background is the main pyramid, known as El Castillo (The Castle). Like Temple I at Tikal, the pyramid has nine terraces, one for each of the lords of the underworld.

Below left Detail of terracing from the Castillo at Chichén. Although the Castillo is less than one-third of the height of Tikal's Temple IV, the sloping sides to each terrace have been deliberately designed to maximize the impression of considerable size.

Right View up the main stairway of the Castillo. Each side has a stairway, and in total there is one step for each day of the year.

Mexicanized, through trading contacts with the Toltecs. There is even evidence of a reverse influence from paintings at Cacaxtla, near Puebla in the Mexican highlands, suggesting that Maya influence reached the area in the Late Classic era, presumably from a Chontal trading-post. A close relationship between the Toltecs and the Chontal was clearly in force. Toltec warriors, perhaps mercenaries, seem to have participated in the takeover of the Yucatán by the Itzá, who can now be identified as a Chontal Maya tribe. Yucatecan chronicles record the commander's title as 'Feathered Serpent' – Quetzalcoatl to the Mexicans, Kukulcan to the Maya. Thus a distinctive hybrid Maya-Toltec style emerged, one which was to become more Mayanized over the years.

The dominant site of this period was Chichén Itzá, founded around AD 950 at what had been a minor centre. The other centres of the Yucatán were not taken over by the Itzá, but recognized their dominance. The architecture of Chichén Itzá greatly resembled that of the Toltec, but with a few exceptions the influence did not spread around the Yucatán. The Itzá were never popular with the true Maya, who resented their dominance. Chichén Itzá itself fell in 1221 to an alliance of Yucatecan forces led by the ruler of Mayapán, a city some 60 miles west of Chichén Itzá. The Itzá, driven from the Yucatán, migrated south to the Petén. They made their new home at Tayasal, a lake island deep in the forest, almost certainly the site of the modern city of Flores on Lake Petén. Tayasal was to remain an outpost of Maya independence long after all others had fallen to the Spanish conquerors.

For the next two and a half centuries Mayapan remained the dominant centre of the Yucatán. It was a fortified city surrounded by a dry stone rampart, a reflection of troubled times. Despite its population of over 15,000 and its dominant position, the architecture is no more than a poor and scaled-down imitation of Chichén Itzá. While the forms and motifs are Toltec, the building techniques are indigenous, and the quality of stone work is distinctly second rate. Mayapan itself and its ruling Cocom dynasty fell to a revolt around 1441 staged by the rival Xiu lineage. The archaeological evidence shows that the city was looted and burnt, and its inhabitants slaughtered.

Following the fall of Mayapan, no leading power emerged in the Yucatán. This was a time of conflict between cities, and of fierce dynastic rivalries. Yet individual cities continued to flourish, such as the beautiful Tulum on the Caribbean coast. This was almost certainly the centre admired by members a Spanish expedition in 1518: 'toward sunset we perceived a city or town so large, that Seville would not have seemed more considerable nor better . . . the same day we came to a beach near which was the highest tower we had seen'.

The Spanish Conquest

It was this fragmented collection of warring states that awaited the Spanish conquistadors. This was not entirely to the Spanish advantage, as the Maya were used to warfare, and there was no overall ruler to be captured, as was the fate of Montezuma, the Aztec emperor. The lack of gold in the Yucatán was a further disincentive for the conquerors. But whatever the reasons, the Maya were among the most fierce and resilient of all the peoples of the New World in the face of conquest.

Following the sighting of an ocean-going canoe in the Gulf of Honduras on Columbus' final voyage, the first significant contact between the Maya and the Spanish was in 1511. A small ship set out that year from the colony of Cuba, only to sink near Jamaica. After two weeks, twelve survivors were washed up on the Yucatán coast. The local chief sacrificed five of them, the remainder escaping to be enslaved by a neighbouring chief. All but two died, one escaping south to Chetumal, where he married the ruler's daughter, and resisted future efforts of the Spanish to persuade him to return. The other was rescued by Cortés on his expedition of 1519, and served him as interpreter.

In 1515 and 1516 a great epidemic of a fatal new disease, perhaps smallpox, swept the Maya. The 'easy death', to which the Maya had no resistance, left a much enfeebled population to meet the Spanish. In spite of this, the Maya were able to fight off a well-armed slave raiding expedition of 1517 near Campeche, following an initial landing on Isla Mujeres. The retreating Spanish resolved to return, their imaginations seized with visions of fabulous wealth, based on the few gold trinkets they had found.

As with other indigenous peoples of the New World, the significance of these events escaped the Maya until it was too late. A second expedition followed in 1518, aiming, although unsuccessfully, to avenge the earlier humiliation. In 1519, Hernán Cortés set sail from Cuba with an expedition of eleven ships and some 500 fighting men. After landing on Cozumel and destroying a few idols and temples,

Left A reclining 'chacmool' sculpture at the top of the main stair to the Temple of the Warriors at Chichén Itzá. Similar examples of these sinister figures have been found elsewhere in Mesoamerica, although not at Classic Maya sites. The plate held on the belly of the reclining man may have been used to hold the hearts of sacrificed victims, or possibly for a torch of flaming oil. On each side of the chacmool stand columns in the form of feathered serpents, which originally held wooden lintels to support the temple roof.

Above right Detail of a warrior's head adorning the platform of the Observatory at Chichén.

Above far right Bas-relief of a jaguar about to devour a sacrificed human heart, on the Platform of the Jaguar and Eagles at Chichén. Both animals represented warrior fraternities, and such militaristic themes are common at Chichén.

Below right Small figures holding up an altar platform at the rear of Chichén's Temple of the Warriors.

Cortés sailed round the peninsula to near the modern city of Veracruz, and marched to the heart of the Aztec empire in the Valley of Mexico. The conquest of the Aztec capital, Tenochtitlán, and most of Central Mexico, was complete by 1521. Despite the small number of conquistadors, the Aztecs and their allies were no match for the combination of European military technology, devastating new diseases, and the skill of the invaders at exploiting traditional rivalries.

By 1523 Cortés was ready to turn his attention towards the Maya, sending his second-in-command, Pedro de Alvarado, in charge of a well-armed 'truth learning' mission to the Guatemala highlands. After a number of battles with the Quiché Maya, de Alvarado was joined by their old enemies the Cakchiquel, and victory soon followed. With the highlands apparently pacified, de Alvarado moved on to conquer the lowlands of modern Salvador, returning to found a city at Iximché. The Cakchiquel soon realized that their new allies posed a terrible threat, and rebelled, destroying the new city. Bitter fighting continued for four years, until finally the Maya chiefs had been crushed. In the process, the highlands were laid waste, and de Alvarado's appalling cruelty had become notorious even among the Spanish.

In 1525 Cortés himself marched with 3,000 men right through the Maya lowlands on his way to put down a rebellion in Honduras by a party of conquistadors. On his way, he made a peaceful visit to the Itzá capital of Tayasal, where mass was celebrated, and he was obliged to leave an injured horse.

No attempt at conquest was made at this stage, either in the Yucatán or the lowlands, although some local chiefs offered allegiance to the Spanish crown. In 1527, Francisco de Montejo left Spain with a royal warrant to colonize the Yucatán. Although he won various battles, de Montejo was eventually forced to leave in 1528, and returned to central Mexico. He returned in 1531, with his son as second-in-command. Again, large areas were subdued, although at considerable cost. By 1535, it was clear that the dramatic Spanish victories over the Incas of Peru and the Aztecs were not to be repeated in the Yucatán, and there were no similar treasures of gold to be won; the Spanish army again withdrew.

Five years later, in 1540, the younger de Montejo returned, finally meeting with greater success. In 1546 a last uprising in the eastern half of the peninsula was put down, and the lands were divided among the

Above The cenote (sacred well) at Chichén Itzá. The whole Yucatán peninsula is formed of limestone, and in many places caves formed by underground rivers have fallen through to form cenotes. Treasures of gold and jade were recovered from the muddy waters, and are now in museums in Mexico City and the United States. Legend has it that beautiful young virgins were laden with finery and cast into the water. The evidence from human remains found there suggests that the elderly and infirm were more likely to have been chosen for sacrifice. Gold was only introduced to Mesoamerica in the tenth century, probably from Panama.

Below Ruined convent in Antigua Guatemala, which became the Spanish capital after the destruction by earthquakes of two earlier attempts to establish a capital. After the construction of numerous churches and monasteries, Antigua was in turn hit by a series of devastating quakes. Colonial architecture proved less earthquake resistant than Maya palaces, and Antigua was eventually abandoned in favour of the present capital.

Left Market place in front of a Catholic church in Chichicastenango in the strongly Mayan highlands of western Guatemala. Although the Maya are nominally Catholic, many elements of older religious practices are preserved in their observances, which include the worship of Maya gods under the guise of local saints, and even the occasional sacrifice of chickens.

Above right Carnival masks on sale in the market at Chichicastenango. The slightly demonic bearded figures represent Spanish conquistadors – folk memories of the devastation they caused live on, even in the twentieth century.

Below right Modern copies of Maya ceramics also in the market at Chichicastenango. At many sites, hopeful lads will try and pass such copies off as the real thing, smeared with a few layers of dirt as a disguise. Professional fakers can produce items which are almost undetectable without scientific dating equipment.

Spanish victors. The Maya peoples became near slaves, working principally on large plantations, underfed and subject to epidemics of European diseases. The achievements of Maya culture were systematically destroyed, their cities quarried for stone to build mansions, monasteries and churches.

By 1546, only the Itzá remained unconquered in their island capital. There was no contact with the Spanish until 1618, when missionaries found that Cortés' abandoned horse was being worshipped as an idol and promptly destroyed it, although they did not persuade the Itzá to accept Christianity. In 1622, the first attempt to conquer Tayasal ended in the massacre of the 160 invaders.

In 1695, a brave Franciscan scholar-priest, Father Avendaño, again reached Tayasal, and failed to persuade the Itzá to accept the Catholic faith. On his return, Avendaño passed through some ruins that were almost certainly Tikal, noting despite his near starvation their different architectural style from the ruins of the Yucatán, and the use of lime plaster over stone masonry. Avendaño was thus the first European to set eyes upon the greatest of the ruined Maya cities.

At last the Spanish could no longer tolerate the Itzá. A 1696 expedition was defeated, but after the completion of a road from the Yucatán to Tayasal in 1697, it was only a matter of time. At dawn on 13 March 1697, after nearly two weeks of hostile manoeuverings by the Itzá and the failure of negotiations, a well-armed Spanish force set out across the lake in a specially-built galley. The Spanish endured a hail of arrows before opening fire with their muskets, killing hundreds of Itzá and routing the remainder.

On entering Tayasal, the conquerors found so many idols that it took until evening to destroy them all. More than 175 years after the fall of the Aztec and Inca empires, the last outpost of Maya independence was finally defeated. The artistic and cultural development of the post-Conquest Itzá was, as far as we know, minimal. But the very existence of an independent Maya state, holding out for nearly two centuries against the might of the conquistadors, was achievement enough.

Early Explorers

The cities and achievements of the Maya were of little interest to most Spanish settlers, who preferred to think of the indigenous peoples as the rebellious descendants of ignorant savages, ungratefully receiving the

Above The island city of Flores, seen along the causeway which links it to the mainland over Lake Petén Itzá. Flores has the only airport in the Petén, and is a staging post for most visitors to Tikal. No Maya ruins have been found around Flores, but it is probably the site of Tayasal, the Maya city that held out against the Spanish conquerors for over 150 years.

Below Double temple platform at the little-visited but finely restored Late Postclassic site of Mixco Viejo, north of Guatemala City. This was the capital of the Pokomam nation, one of the smaller highland Maya peoples. Despite the city's strategic hill-top location, it fell easily to the Spanish under the conquistador de Alvarado, who paid local informers to betray its defensive secrets.

immeasurable benefits of European religion and civilization. This attitude persists among Spanish-speaking people today, many of whom look down on the Maya and other indigenous groups. During the colonial period the more accessible ruins were used as quarries or built over, while in the further-flung jungles and mountains they stood ignored and overgrown.

After the fall of Tayasal, there were regular Maya revolts against the hardships of colonial rule, invariably followed by harsh counter-measures. These continued after the independence of Mexico and Guatemala, with horrific racial wars between Maya and Europeans in the Yucatán continuing into the twentieth century. These led to one fascinating and little-known episode in Tikal's history, when Maya refugees migrated from the Yucatán to Tikal in the 1840s, and reoccupied parts of the site. Much of the defacement of monuments and graffiti is thought to date from this time. A plague of vampire bats apparently drove out the occupiers, perhaps saving monuments from further destruction. The name of Tikal, thought to mean 'Place of the Voices', probably dates from this time.

The pattern of Maya revolts against *ladino* (Spanish-speaking) rule has continued to this day. Even in the 1980s, near-genocidal campaigns by the Guatemalan military against rural insurgents in the Maya highlands can be seen as part of the continuing pattern. Throughout the Maya area today, tensions continue between the indigenous peoples and land-hungry *ladino* settlers, which occasionally culminate in bloodshed.

It was thus against a background of warfare and instability that European explorers first became aware of Maya ruins in the early nineteenth century. The acknowledged fathers of modern Mayanology were John Stephens and Frederick Catherwood, an American lawyer and an English artist. Between 1839 and 1842, the two travelled widely throughout Central America, busily writing, mapping and drawing. Their books were bestsellers, the two volumes of *Incidents of Travel in Central America, Chiapas, and Yucatán* meeting with particular success.

The books are divided between descriptions of the Maya sites, and accounts of various hardships and dangers. The pair's first journey took them from Belize, down through Guatemala to various sites, and back up to Palenque. They did not visit Tikal, although Stephens actually bought the ruins at Copán for a bargain 50 dollars. The second journey concentrated on the sites of the northern Yucatán. They were not the first visitors to these sites, which receive occasional mentions in Spanish chronicles through the colonial period. By the time of their journeys, interest in Mesoamerican studies was stirring in learned antiquarian circles. But the popular success of Stephens' and Catherwood's work marks the beginning of modern Maya studies.

Unlike some of his predecessors, Stephens had no doubt that the ruins he saw were the product of an indigenous civilization, and that they equalled those of other ancient peoples. There was a sense of wonder in his observations:

> Here, as the sculptor worked, he turned to the theatre of his glory, as did the Greek to the Acropolis of Athens, and dreamed of immortal fame. Little did he imagine that the time would come when his works would perish, his race would be extinct, his city a desolation and abode for reptiles, for strangers to gaze at and wonder by which race it had once been inhabited.

Explorers, archaeologists and scholars followed them in increasing numbers. The challenge of deciphering Maya glyphic writing and the calendar was a particular attraction. It took many years for New World studies to achieve full intellectual respectability, given the narrow emphasis of the archaeological establishment on the world of classical antiquity. This attitude persists, especially in Europe, to this day.

The first visitor to Tikal in this phase of Maya studies was a Swiss explorer, Dr Gustav Bernoulli, who in 1877 explored the site and arranged for the removal of various of the carved wooden lintels from the temples. He was followed by English ex-diplomat, Alfred Maudsley, who began with casual explorations, but soon acquired a great passion for the excavation and recording of Maya ruins. During the 1880s and 90s, he made numerous visits to all of the known Maya sites. His photographs and meticulous drawings of Tikal, where he cleared Temple I, are still referred to by archaeologists.

Tikal was first mapped fully around the same time by an Austrian explorer, Teobert Maler. He was sponsored in his travels by the Peabody Museum of Harvard, with which he eventually quarrelled, and the map was never published. The final key figure in Tikal's history from this age of individual explorers was Sylvanus Morley, who visited

Above The main temple at Tulum, a Late Postclassic Maya city, and one of the few still occupied at the time of the Spanish Conquest. Although Tulum is one of the most beautiful Maya sites, given its unique position on the Caribbean, architecturally it is of little note.

Above right General view of the central complex at Tulum. The city was surrounded on three sides by walls, and on the fourth by the sea, reflecting the turbulence of the Postclassic era. This was one of the first cities to be seen by Spanish explorers, who remarked on its beauty.

Below right The recently restored Court of the Thousand Columns at Chichén Itzá, apparently the residential quarters of an élite warrior cult. Such large restoration projects are expensive, but the numbers of tourists visiting the site make it an economic proposition. Tikal desperately needs similar investment, but until Guatemala can solve its political and economic problems, this remains unlikely.

Above The bus station at Flores in the Petén, dusty, hot and crowded. Maya and Spanish-speaking people from all over Guatemala are moving into the Petén, desperate for land. The rate and scale of colonization threatens both environmental and social disaster. The rich rainforest that sustained Tikal's multitudes over many centuries will disappear within a single lifetime unless urgent action is taken for its protection.

Below Restoration underway at Copán in Honduras, on a scale which Tikal has not seen for 20 years or more. As archaeology becomes an increasingly accurate science, the element of guess-work is eliminated from such reconstructions.

Tikal on numerous occasions between the two world wars, and for whom the deciphering of hieroglyphs was a consuming obsession. His great work, *The Ancient Maya*, now updated to reflect the latest state of knowledge, is still the most comprehensive and readable account of the Maya available.

Modern Excavations

The next phase of Mayanology sees institutions, mainly American universities, playing a greater role in sponsoring excavation and restoration projects. At Tikal, the University of Pennsylvania carried out the largest project of all, the Tikal Project, between 1955 and 1966. Teams of archaeologists, with hundreds of labourers, excavated most of the central zone and mapped the whole surrounding area. During this period, for the first time, restoration was carried out deliberately for the purpose of encouraging tourism, to be an increasingly important factor.

Despite the scale of resources devoted to these large-scale projects, by the 1960s there remained large gaps in knowledge of the Maya, and fundamental disagreements between respected scholars. Work on deciphering glyphs and establishing the exact correlation between the Maya and Gregorian calendar had advanced considerably, but was still not conclusive. Relatively little was established beyond doubt concerning patterns of human settlement, movements of peoples, trade routes and the precise chronology of events.

More recent studies have been on a smaller scale, using sophisticated scientific methods to solve targetted problems. Work divides into a number of distinct areas. Conventional excavation of sites continues, with Guatemalan and Mexican archaeologists playing an increasingly important role. The Maya calendar is now understood, while glyph decipherment has only a few remaining unanswered questions. This has allowed considerable advance on the historical side; the names and dates of Maya rulers, and events during their reigns, are now known in some cities, not least at Tikal, although gaps remain.

However, the greatest current advances are in the related studies of human settlement, economics and agricultural ecology. The use of computers and molecular analysis means that even one isolated pottery fragment can provide valuable information, perhaps providing trading links between cities at a certain period, or allowing the precise dating of a building where it is found. The analysis of pollen from lake-bed soil cores can show which plants were under cultivation. Satellite photography is another valuable tool, but the best results are obtained where these different disciplines are combined to tackle a particular problem.

At the same time, archaeologists face new obstacles to their work, most with their roots in the economics of poverty. Grave-robbing, for centuries a way of supplementing rural incomes, has now become a major industry. Fuelled by the greed of secret 'collectors' in the United States and other countries, robbers are now mechanized, heavily armed and ruthless. Whole sites are ransacked or even bulldozed in search of a few precious relics, instantly destroying the evidence of centuries. Officials are corrupted by the huge bribes on offer, while archaeologists and local people have been murdered. Great carved stelae have been dismembered with mechanical cutters, and carted off in pieces for sale to the highest bidder.

The jungle itself is under threat as the land-hungry poor and cattle ranchers compete to clear forest. Loggers, some entering illegally from Mexico, devastate huge areas to extract hardwoods. Unique and fragile ecosystems rapidly disappear, giving way to soil erosion and pollution. Political discontent among the deprived and militarization are additional destabilizing factors in the Petén. Massacres of settler communities were carried out by the military during the civil war of the early 1980s. The 220 square miles of the Tikal National Park seem safe for the time being, but may soon become a small island of forest surrounded by a greatly degraded environment.

No major excavations are currently underway at Tikal, and none are likely, given Guatemala's current economic crisis. Even conservation work has largely stopped, and only routine unskilled maintenance can be carried out. There are plans for an ambitious reconstruction of Temple I, always scheduled for next year, but always postponed through lack of funds. Acid rain and the destructive effects of tourism are now damaging stucco facings and delicate stone carvings. Although Tikal's survival is not threatened, much will soon be lost without a major new inflow of funds and effort. Paradoxically, this will only come if tourists can be attracted in far greater numbers than at present,

The classic view of Temple I at Tikal, facing over the Great Plaza. The temple was heavily restored by the Tikal Project during the 1960s, but now needs major works to ensure its continued preservation as one of the world's great archaeological monuments.

as they are to the great (and well-serviced) sites in the Yucatán; thousands in a day visit Chichén Itzá and Uxmal alone.

One reason for hope is the plan to create a 'Maya Route', linking all the principal Maya ruins in Mexico, Guatemala, Belize and Honduras. Co-operation between five governments in a part of the world that combines political instability with astonishing levels of bureaucracy is difficult, and investment in the necessary infrastructure and facilities will be hard to attract. Conversely, success would threaten Tikal's remote magic, with the awful prospect of becoming the star attraction in the Mayaland Theme Park. But all these worries seem far away as dusk falls in Tikal, the Place of Voices, and bats swoop around the temples of the Great Plaza, their thin cries echoing like the voices of Maya ghosts, as the golden light of the setting sun fades to darkness.

Travellers' Information

Planning the trip

When to go
The heavy rainy season, which lasts from June to November or mid-December, makes land travel difficult, leaves trails through the ruins muddy, and the ruins themselves slippery. Tikal is best visited between mid-December and May, when mosquito life is also relatively subdued. Temperatures are high throughout the year, normally in the range 25–30°C (77–86°F), but cooler in the winter months.

Travel documents
For citizens of most countries, including Britain and the USA, no visa is necessary. A Tourist Card, valid for 30 days, is issued on arrival at any international airport. It is advisable to obtain a Tourist Card in advance from any Guatemalan Embassy or Consulate if arriving by land.

Insurance
While the risks of theft and illness are lower than in many other Latin American countries, travel insurance is necessary. Cover should include repatriation in case of medical emergency, theft of cash and valuables, and flight delay (especially in the rainy season). In the unlikely case of severe illness or injury, repatriation is the best option.

Costs and money
The Guatemalan currency is the Quetzal, which is divided into 100 centavos. Exchange rates offered at Tikal are poor, so it is better to change money in Flores or Guatemala City. Travellers cheques are difficult to negotiate outside big cities, so be sure to take a good supply of cash US dollars, with a mix of large and smaller bills, which are widely accepted. Credit cards are only useful for air tickets and a few up-market establishments.

Guatemala is a cheap country. A budget traveller can survive on approximately US$50 a week, but it is easy to spend more in a day, especially at Tikal, a relatively expensive area.

Health precautions
Most visitors to Tikal experience no health problems other than from the wide range of biting insects, which may be partly discouraged by repellents. Ticks can be removed by heat treatment with a lighted cigarette. Malaria is found in the area, so it is necessary to take the right preventative medicine.

Stomach problems are a possibility, reduced by sensible precautions: keeping hands clean; drinking only bottled water, soft drinks and beer; avoiding dehydration; eating only peeled fruit; making sure all other food is fresh and well cooked. In the event of diarrhoea, drink lots of clean water or soft drinks and eat sparingly. If more serious symptoms develop or if the illness persists, consult a doctor or pharmacist.

Clothes and equipment
No specialist equipment is required to visit Tikal. Clothing should be light and suited to a tropical environment. Long sleeves and trousers are advisable to protect against sun and insects. Take sun-screen lotion and insect repellent. Waterproofs are essential in the rainy season, as are solid shoes with a good grip. A torch (flashlight) is useful at the ruins. Military-style equipment and camouflage clothing should not be taken, to avoid the possibility of misunderstandings.

Organized tours
A number of companies in Europe and North America offer tours to Mexico and Guatemala which include a visit to Tikal. Among the best British companies are Virgin Holidays (tel: [Crawley] 0293-775511) and Journey Latin America (tel: [London] 081-747-8315).

Travel to and near Tikal

By air

The most popular route to Tikal is by air from Guatemala City via Santa Elena airport at Flores. This service is provided daily by the Guatemalan airlines Aerovias, Aviateca, Aeroquetzal and Tapsa, at a single fare of about $50. Most departures are around 7 a.m., returning around 4 p.m., to cater for day-trippers. Five days a week, the Aerovias plane continues to Belize City, returning to Guatemala City via Flores. At the time of writing there are no direct flights from Mexico, but a service may soon be launched between Cancún and Flores.

By road

Tikal is connected to Flores, capital of the Petén, by the state's only paved road, a distance of some 40 miles (65 km). The bus service on this road is inadequate, with a few slow and crowded buses a day, so travellers are advised to use one of the many private minibus ('combi') services; these are provided by many hotels, and there is a direct service from the airport.

Flores is connected to the outside world by three rough dirt roads, all of which are impassable for much of the rainy season. They are not recommended for cars or small vehicles, even those with 4-wheel drive. The main road to Flores runs north-west from Río Dulce, some 190 miles (300 km) from Guatemala City by paved road. The unpaved Flores road is only a further 125 miles (200 km), but the overall journey by bus can easily take 16-24 hours. There are regular services from the capital.

A second Flores-Guatemala City route is via Sayaxché and Coban. This road is also rough and hazards include uncertain bus services, with possible military and guerilla activity. Flores is also accessible from Belize, on a partly paved road of 125 miles (200 km). There are some direct buses to Flores via Belize from Chetumal in Mexico.

Through the jungle

There are two road and river routes to Flores from Palenque in Mexico, which offer the possibility of visiting Maya ruins en route, but are only for the adventurous, and have inconvenient timetables involving dawn departures. River travel is either by slow and cheap cargo boat, or by faster but expensive hired launch. These journeys are best embarked upon with a small supply of food and water, a hammock, blanket or light sleeping-bag, and perhaps a mosquito net.

The most travelled route is on the northerly Río San Pedro. Buses run from Palenque via Tenosique to the river port of La Palma. There is a daily boat service (4–5 hours) to El Naranjo, an unattractive Guatemalan garrison town. El Naranjo is served by two buses a day to Flores, a very rough 85 miles (120 km) on a dirt road.

A more interesting route is via Sayaxché, on the Río de la Pasión 40 miles (60 km) south-west of Flores. There are frequent buses between Sayaxché and Flores on an unpaved road. There are two possible ports in Mexico, Benemérito and Corazal, both with basic inns, and both served by at least one daily bus along the dirt road that runs south-east from Palenque; this journey can take 12 hours. Corazal is close to the superb ruins of Yaxchilán, on the Mexican side of the Usumacinta, about 45 minutes boat ride downstream. It takes a day to travel upstream between Yaxchilán and Sayaxché by launch. First there is a Guatemalan military checkpoint where papers are checked. A little further on, the ruins of Altar de Sacrificios are worth a quick visit.

Ruins near Tikal

Although the region around Tikal has numerous Maya ruins, most are difficult to get to, and being largely unrestored, offer little to look at beyond mounds of rubble in the jungle. The tourist office in Flores (at the airport) has up-to-date information about sites near Tikal, and recommends guides and tour operators.

Uaxactún

Uaxactún is a well-known site 15 miles (24 km) north of Tikal, occupied from the Preclassic right through to Classic times. It is reached along a dirt road, only passable by vehicle in the dry season. Walking takes about 6 hours, so an overnight stay is unavoidable. Food and hammock space is available at the village near the ruins. The path can be hard to follow, and a guide is recommended.

Around Sayaxché

There is an interesting cluster of minor but historically significant ruins near Sayaxché, 40 miles (60 km) south-west of Flores, all accessible by river. Sayaxché itself is a pleasant backwater. The local English-speaking entrepreneurs offer boat trips to the ruins, but for about 50 per cent more than the going rate at the waterfront; expect to pay around $20–25 per day (per boat), with only a modest surcharge for many passengers. Make sure the boat has a palm roof to protect from sun and rain.

The principal ruins near Sayaxché are Seibal (also accessible by road), Aguateca and Dos Pilas, each of which may be reached on a day trip. Of these, Seibal is the most impressive and accessible, lying half an hour's walk through the forest from the Río de la Pasión an hour or two upstream from Sayaxché. There is one principal restored temple, surrounded by well-preserved stelae. Aguateca and Dos Pilas are in the forest near Lake Petexbatún, some 6 miles (10 km) south of Sayaxché up a small tributary of the Río de la Pasión. Dos Pilas, west of the lake, is best visited in the dry season, owing to otherwise heavy mud along much of the 8 mile (12 km) path. Aguateca is an easy hour's walk from the south of the lake into the hills above.

Ruins en route to Tikal

Copán (Honduras)

Those going by land to Tikal from Guatemala City should visit the superb ruins of Copán just over the border in Honduras. These are reached in about 5 hours bus travel from Guatemala City; take a direct bus to Chiquimula (2½ hours), then change to a bus to the frontier post at El Florido (1½ hours by dirt road). Here you can obtain a temporary pass out from Guatemala to visit the ruins. The pleasant small town of Copán, with various hotels, is about half an hour away by minibus, and the ruins about 20 minutes walk further on. The Honduran currency, the Lempira, is similar in value and buying power to the Quetzal; currency is freely traded at the frontier.

Quiriguá

Quiriguá is another island of ruins and forest, this time surrounded by a vast banana plantation. Most make the journey by bus from Guatemala City. From the roadside stop, it is about 2 miles (3 km) to the ruins; motorbike taxis make the trip. Quiriguá is known not for its structures (of which little remain), but for its many towering, excellently preserved stelae, the most spectacular in the Maya world.

Yaxchilán and Bonampak (Mexico)

Yaxchilán and Bonampak may both be visited between Tikal and Palenque by those taking the river route (see above). Yaxchilán, situated on a strategic loop in the Usumacinta, is one of the finest lowland Maya sites, and little visited due to its inaccessibility. Those who do make the trip will be well rewarded. There is a reasonable comedor on site, and palapas under which to sling a hammock; campers are welcome.

Bonampak, famous for its wall paintings, is harder to get to, involving a half-day trek through the jungle. If this sounds like too much effort, visit the replica in Mexico City's Museum of Anthropology. There is another way to get to Yaxchilán and Bonampak – light aircraft can be engaged in Palenque, San Cristóbal and Ocosingo, to visit both sites on a day trip. Expect to pay about $120 per person, 3 to a plane.

Where to stay and eat

Tikal and Flores

In general, it is best to stay at Tikal itself to have the maximum time to spend at the ruins. However, there are some good hotels outside the National Park, and many may need to stay in Flores for transport connections.

There are any number of cheap hotels in Santa Elena and Flores, none exactly recommendable. Perhaps the best hotel in Flores is the Savanna (tel: [Flores] 081-1248, or 2-940-295 in Guatemala City), built right over the water and with its own private island on the lake; the nearby Petén (tel: 1692) and Yum Kax (tel: 1692) also offer reasonable facilities.

There are several hotels at Tikal itself, just outside the archaeological zone; as there is no phone link into the park, all bookings are handled outside. The largest hotel is the Jungle Lodge (tel: [Guatemala City] 2-760-294), which offers well-constructed modern bungalows. The smaller Tikal Inn is another good choice. There is also a camp-site that is fine for those with the equipment and not too fussy about regular showers.

At the time of writing, a new luxury hotel, the Camino Real, is under construction just outside the National Park on the banks of Lago Petén Itzá, which will be the most expensive accommodation in the Petén. For a more relaxed atmosphere, an 'ecological' hotel on the lake between Flores and Tikal is El Gringo Perdido (tel: [Guatemala City] 2-323-802).

Eating in Tikal is not a problem, as there are a number of comedors (cheap restaurants) serving basic meals. Eating well is a tougher proposition: one establishment which sets out to provide a higher standard of cuisine is the Jaguar Inn, yet the food on offer is remarkably similar to the comedors. Resign yourself to plenty of wholesome beans, tortillas, eggs and chicken.

Sayaxché

Sayaxché has a comfortable, friendly hotel, the Guayacan, right by the waterfront to the Río de la Pasión. There is just one acceptable restaurant, which is actually rather good: the Yax-Kin, just around the corner from the hotel. The owner is a good source of information about the area.

General information

Information

There is a helpful tourist information office at Flores' Santa Elena airport (closed on Mondays).

Time zones

Guatemala, Mexico, Belize and Honduras are all on Central Standard Time, GMT minus 6 hours; there is no daylight saving time.

Laws and regulations

Most tourists have no problems, but should carry passport and Tourist Card at all times, and avoid possession of illegal drugs or archaeological finds.

Access to museums and sites

Most sites and museums are open daily, from 9 a.m. to 5 p.m., with low entrance charges. Most of the remoter sites make no charge. Those wishing to remain in Tikal after 5 p.m. should obtain a special stamp on their pass (no charge) from the guardpost near the entrance to the ruins.

Photography

An ultra-violet 'daylight' filter is essential to accommodate the strong light. A limited selection of film is available, but it is better to bring enough of your own. Be sensitive about taking pictures of local people, who may refuse to be photographed or request a tip.

Personal security

This is not usually a problem for tourists in Guatemala, although thieves are active in bus stations and crowds. When in discussion with police, guerrillas or military, it is advisable to smile and obey orders.

Electric current

As in the USA, electricity in Central America is supplied at nominal 110V 60Hz. Supply is variable, and 220V is occasionally encountered.

Communications

There is a telephone (Guatel) office in Santa Elena, where there is a long wait for an expensive telephone service to the USA, and sometimes to other countries. There are no phones within the Tikal National Park. There are no fax or telex lines available. There is however an on-site post office at Tikal, as well as offices in Flores and Santa Elena. Most letters sent arrive sooner or later.

Embassy addresses

UK Guatemalan Embassy: 13 Fawcett St, London SW10 9HN. (tel: 071-351-3042).

UK Mexican Embassy: 8 Halkin Street, London SW1. (tel: 071-235-6393).

UK Belize High Commission: 200 Sutherland Av, London W9. (tel: 071-226-3485).

British Embassies

Guatemala: 7 Avenida 5-10, 7th Floor, Zona 4. (tel: 2-321-601).

Belize: Half Moon Av, Belmopan. (tel: 08-22146).

Mexico: Río Lerma 71, Zona 6. (tel: 5-511-4880).

Further reading

History and Culture

The Maya, Michael D. Coe, Thames and Hudson, London, 1987. A short and very readable account of Maya society and history; updated in line with latest discoveries.

Incidents of Travel in Central America, Chiapas and Yucatán, John L. Stephens, Century, London 1988. Vivid account of travels in the Maya region in the turbulent nineteenth century.

Ancient Maya Civilization, Norman Hammond, Rutgers University Press, New Jersey, 1988. Scholarly but clear summary of current Mayanist thinking.

The Ancient Maya, Sylvanus Morley (rev. 1983 Robert Sharer), Stanford 1983. The definitive guide to all aspects of Maya culture and archaeology.

View from the Top of the Temple, Kenneth Pearce, University of New Mexico, 1984.

The Classic Maya Collapse, ed. Patrick Culbert, University of New Mexico, 1983. A collection of academic essays, explaining the latest theories about the Maya collapse.

Guidebooks

Tikal – A Handbook of the Ancient Maya Ruins, William R. Coe, University of Pennsylvania, reprinted annually. The definitive stone by stone guide to the ruins.

A Guide to Ancient Maya Ruins, Bruce Hunter, Univ. of Oklahoma Press, 1986. Archaeological guide to the major Maya sites, for serious travellers.

The Rough Guide to Guatemala and Belize, Harrap, London, reprinted annually. A useful practical guide to getting around, eating and sleeping.

The Rulers of Tikal, Genevieve Michel, Vista Publications, Guatemala, reprinted annually. An invaluable field guide to the stelae of Tikal.

Chronology

Prehistory and Archaic Era

*c.*30,000 BC First evidence (disputed) of humans in the Americas

*c.*7000 BC End of Ice Age in the Americas.

*c.*3000 BC Cultivation of maize in Mesoamerica, allowing development of settled societies.

*c.*2000 BC Proto-Mayan language in use over most of Maya area.

Preclassic Era

2000 BC– AD 150 Village agriculture throughout Maya area, from coast and up rivers. Pottery and stone tools in widespread use. Stone temples built.

*c.*1000 BC Sophisticated Olmec civilization in south-east Mexico at its height. Strong influence on Maya area. Mayan Izapa culture develops in rainforests of Guatemala.

*c.*100 BC Sophisticated Maya calendar evolved to near-final form, based on Olmec original.

Early Classic Era

*c.*250–900 Golden Age of the Maya, especially in area of Tikal. Widespread trade throughout Mesoamerica.

*c.*278 First dated monument at Tikal.

*c.*292 First identified ruler of Tikal, Scroll Ahau Jaguar, probably fifth ruler in dynastic line.

*c.*300 Flowering of Teotihuacán culture in Valley of Mexico. Teotihuacán domination of Maya highlands, with major satellite at Kaminaljuya.

*c.*317 Jaguar Paw I becomes ruler of Tikal, first of several rulers with variants on the same name.

*c.*376 Jaguar Paw II ruling at Tikal. Uaxactún and other nearby cities fall under Tikal influence.

*c.*379 Curl Nose, possibly from Teotihuacán, becomes ruler of Tikal.

*c.*426 Stormy Sky becomes ruler of Tikal, and establishes dominance over the Maya lowlands.

*c.*475 Kan Boar becomes ruler of Tikal; austere architectural style in evidence.

*c.*537 Double Bird becomes ruler of Tikal. Hiatus in artistic production and temple building, lasting some 50 years.

Late Classic Era

*c.*600 Collapse of Teotihuacán, precipitated by barbarian invasion from the north. Tikal at its height, with up to 50,000 inhabitants.

*c.*682 Ah Cacau Caan Chac becomes ruler of Tikal. Extensive building and evidence of prosperity.

*c.*734 Yax Kin Caan Chac succeeds his father Ah Cacau, building the enormous Temple IV.

*c.*750 Decline of trade, and increased conflict between Maya cities.

*c.*751 Accession of last known ruler of Tikal, Chitam.

*c.*790–*c.*830 Apocalypse of Classic Maya cities. Agricultural and economic collapse leads to depopulation, and abandonment of most cities.

Post-Classic Era

*c.*1000 Toltecs from the Valley of Mexico extend influence in Yucatán. Evolution of new Maya-Toltec culture, the Itzá.

*c.*1224 Itzá driven out of Chichén Itzá by forces of Mayapan, settling in the Petén. City of Mayapan dominates peninsula for two centuries.

1345 Founding of aggressively expansionist Aztec state in Valley of Mexico. Trading links with Maya develop.

*c.*1450 Revolt leads to fall of Mayapan. Frequent civil wars between cities in the Yucatán.

1492 Christopher Columbus lands in the Americas.

1511 Spanish ship wrecked on the Yucatán coast; one sailor becomes local chieftain.

1512–18 Spanish expeditions explore Maya coast.

1519 Hernan Cortés lands near modern Veracruz, with 500 conquistadors.

Spanish Conquest

1521	Final fall of the Aztec capital to Cortés. Central Mexico swiftly conquered.
1523	De Alvarado commences conquest of Maya highlands.
1524	Cortés leads exploratory expedition passing near Tikal.
1527	Spanish subjugation of the Yucatán begins under de Montejo.
1546	Final Maya uprising crushed; most resistance now over.
1562	Bishop Diego de Landa orders the mass burning of Maya manuscripts at Maní in the Yucatán.
1598	Colonization of modern Mexico and Guatemala complete; population largely enslaved, and subject to devastating epidemics of European diseases.
1695/6	Spanish expedition under Father Avendaño reaches Tikal.
1697	Fall of Tayasal, last Itzá Maya outpost in the Petén, to the Spanish. Frequent rebellions continue.

Independence and Early Explorations

1821	Mexican and Guatemalan independence from Spain.
1839–42	American lawyer John Stephens and English artist Frederick Catherwood undertake journeys of discovery to Maya sites. Civil wars and rebellions throughout Central America.
1842	Spanish-descended Yucatecos declare independence. Yucatán (unsuccessfully) seeks statehood in USA.
1847–1855	Yucatán War of the Castes, a brutal racial conflict between Maya and Europeans, ending in Maya defeat. Maya refugees settle at Tikal. Various monuments defaced. Plague of vampire bats eventually drives settlers from area.
1848	Rediscovery of Tikal by Spanish explorers.
1858	Maya religious uprising in the Yucatán; Europeans massacred. Mexican army finally reconquers area in 1901.

1877	Swiss explorer, Dr Gustav Bernoulli, visits Tikal, and arranges for removal of carved wooden lintels.
1880s	English archaeologist and photographer Alfred Maudslay clears and maps parts of Tikal.
1895	German explorer, Teobert Maler, visits Tikal, returning in 1904.

Modern Times

1901	Maya rebellion in Quintana Roo against Mexican dictatorship.
1914–28	Sylvanus Morley, the father of modern Maya studies, makes frequent visits to the Petén and Tikal.
1944	Major Cakchiquel Maya rebellion in Guatemalan highlands.
1946	Discovery of Bonampak by American travellers.
1951	Government committed to agrarian reform elected in Guatemala; land redistribution starts in favour of Maya communities. American-backed invasion and coup follow in 1954; land reform reversed.
1956	Tikal Project begins; major excavations under the University of Pennsylvania.
1966–69	State of siege in much of Guatemala; many thousand civilians die in counter-insurgency campaign.
1971	Tikal Project concludes main work; excavations continue under Guatemalan auspices.
1980s	Civil War in highland Maya and other areas. Widespread atrocities by Guatemalan military, principally against Maya communities. Many refugees in camps along Mexican border.
1991	Guatemala in economic crisis but largely at peace following elections, with insurgency contained to remote areas; army and police death squads continue to murder peasant leaders, trades unionists, homeless children and others.

Index